JUMBLE®
Getaway

Your Ticket to a Paradise of Puzzles!

Henri Arnold,
Bob Lee,
and
Mike Argirion

TRIUMPH
BOOKS

Jumble® is a registered trademark
of Tribune Media Services, Inc.

Copyright © 2011 by Tribune Media Services, Inc.
All rights reserved.

Triumph Books and colophon are registered trademarks of
Random House, Inc.

This book is available in quantity at special discounts
for your group or organization.

For further information, contact:

Triumph Books
542 South Dearborn Street
Suite 750
Chicago, Illinois 60605
(312) 939-3330
Fax (312) 663-3557
www.triumphbooks.com

Printed in U.S.A.

ISBN: 978-1-60078-547-4

Design by Sue Knopf

Contents

JUMBLE®

Getaway

Classic Puzzles

JUMBLE®

Unscramble these four Jumbles, one letter to
each square, to form four ordinary words.

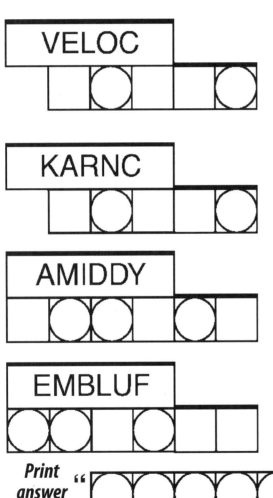

VELOC

KARNC

AMIDDY

EMBLUF

I need a
rest. Yuck!
This is
awful

HOW THE MECHANIC
DESCRIBED THE
COFFEE.

Now arrange the circled letters to form the
surprise answer, as suggested by the above
cartoon.

*Print
answer
here*   " ◯◯◯◯◯ " ◯◯◯◯◯

JUMBLE®

Unscramble these four Jumbles, one letter to each square, to form four ordinary words.

KNUSK

WARLD

BLOWEB

BELTOT

Caught him red-handed, Sarge

WHAT HAPPENED TO THE LIBRARY THIEF?

Now arrange the circled letters to form the surprise answer, as suggested by the above cartoon.

Print answer here   HE 〇〇〇 " 〇〇〇〇〇〇 "

JUMBLE®

Unscramble these four Jumbles, one letter to each square, to form four ordinary words.

YOPEN

ARLAT

TAILIC

WELBIA

It wasn't me

You were the only one here

NOT TELLING THE TRUTH CAN BE——

Now arrange the circled letters to form the surprise answer, as suggested by the above cartoon.

Print answer **A** *here*

JUMBLE®

Unscramble these four Jumbles, one letter to each square, to form four ordinary words.

POEMT

TALVE

WHACES

ENPLYT

Gotcha!   I was just looking at it

WHAT THE SHOP-
LIFTER GOT WHEN
HE TOOK THE
FANCY CALENDAR.

Now arrange the circled letters to form the surprise answer, as suggested by the above cartoon.

Print answer here

JUMBLE®

Unscramble these four Jumbles, one letter to each square, to form four ordinary words.

CEDID

RUTYL

TUFITO

SLOIPH

You have to sift slowly

WHEN SHE HELPED MOM BAKE A CAKE, SHE TURNED INTO A---

Now arrange the circled letters to form the surprise answer, as suggested by the above cartoon.

Print answer here " ◯◯◯◯◯ " ◯◯◯◯◯

JUMBLE.

Unscramble these four Jumbles, one letter to each square, to form four ordinary words.

BEIPD

CLUHG

BISMUT

PINTUR

That's pretty good

It's all coming back to me

WHAT THE FORMER ARTIST DID WHEN HE RETURNED TO THE EASEL.

Now arrange the circled letters to form the surprise answer, as suggested by the above cartoon.

Print answer here "◯◯◯◯◯◯◯" ◯◯

7

JUMBLE.

Unscramble these four Jumbles, one letter to each square, to form four ordinary words.

RELEC

CARTT

DORFIL

MYDIAS

Hey, look at this over here

WHERE THE TOUR GROUP WENT TO VIEW THE SEA MAMMALS.

Now arrange the circled letters to form the surprise answer, as suggested by the above cartoon.

Print answer THE "⌀⌀⌀⌀⌀" ⌀⌀⌀⌀
here

JUMBLE®

Unscramble these four Jumbles, one letter to
each square, to form four ordinary words.

ULIGE

CETTO

RUTTAN

GLUEDE

Check the bearings.
You're off course

WHAT THE CAPTAIN
GAVE THE NEW
HELMSMAN.

Now arrange the circled letters to form the
surprise answer, as suggested by the above
cartoon.

Print answer here " ◯◯◯◯◯◯◯◯◯ "

JUMBLE®

Unscramble these four Jumbles, one letter to each square, to form four ordinary words.

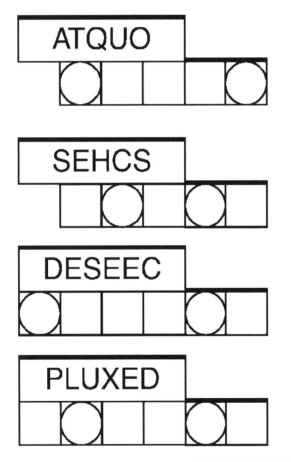

ATQUO

SEHCS

DESEEC

PLUXED

By far, the heaviest ever

WHEN THE PUMPKIN WAS WEIGHED, THE RECORD WAS----

Now arrange the circled letters to form the surprise answer, as suggested by the above cartoon.

Print answer here " "

10

JUMBLE®

Unscramble these four Jumbles, one letter to each square, to form four ordinary words.

DYLOM

FENTO

INGINN

DEGULC

I'm going to enter the day's activities

WHAT THE SHIP'S CAPTAIN DID WHEN HE GOT A COMPUTER.

Now arrange the circled letters to form the surprise answer, as suggested by the above cartoon.

Print answer here " ◯◯◯◯◯◯ " ◯◯

JUMBLE®

Unscramble these four Jumbles, one letter to each square, to form four ordinary words.

PAUNC

LABNK

DOAJIN

KLINTE

We found a
good spot

THE NOVICE DUCK HUNTERS ATTRIB- UTED THEIR SUC- CESS TO ---

Now arrange the circled letters to form the surprise answer, as suggested by the above cartoon.

Print answer here "◯◯◯◯◯◯" ◯◯◯◯

JUMBLE®

Unscramble these four Jumbles, one letter to each square, to form four ordinary words.

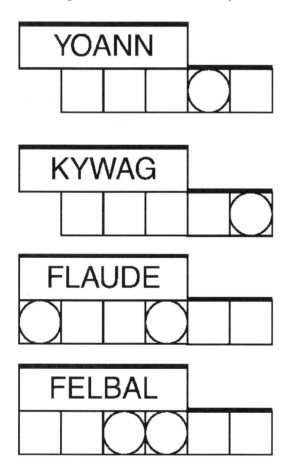

YOANN

KYWAG

FLAUDE

FELBAL

No golf for you today

HIS DAY OFF TURNED INTO THIS WHEN HE WOKE UP WITH A COLD.

Now arrange the circled letters to form the surprise answer, as suggested by the above cartoon.

Print answer here AN ◯◯◯ ◯◯◯

JUMBLE®

Unscramble these four Jumbles, one letter to each square, to form four ordinary words.

DRECY

GLAVE

GODINI

WULTOA

His fifth degree

He's well versed on many ____ subjects

AFTER YEARS OF STUDY, THE PORTLY SCHOLAR WAS----

Now arrange the circled letters to form the surprise answer, as suggested by the above cartoon.

Print answer here

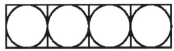 "  "

JUMBLE®

Unscramble these four Jumbles, one letter to each square, to form four ordinary words.

BEGOF

TAMID

KRILLE

RODION

I'll just sit over here

I'll take these, these, these and...

WHAT THE SUGAR DADDY DID WHEN SHE SHOPPED FOR SHOES.

Now arrange the circled letters to form the surprise answer, as suggested by the above cartoon.

Print answer here "  " THE

JUMBLE®

Unscramble these four Jumbles, one letter to each square, to form four ordinary words.

POCUR

SELBS

SHELIC

SLAQUL

This will help reduce the sun's glare

WORN BY THE ROWING TEAM FOR THE BIG RACE.

Now arrange the circled letters to form the surprise answer, as suggested by the above cartoon.

Print answer here " ⬡⬡⬡⬡⬡ " ⬡⬡⬡⬡

JUMBLE®

Unscramble these four Jumbles, one letter to each square, to form four ordinary words.

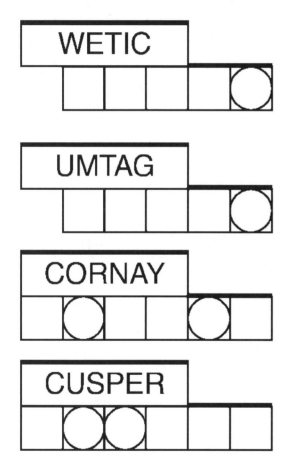

WETIC

UMTAG

CORNAY

CUSPER

You'll need this study for the meeting

THE STATESMAN WAS GIVEN THIS WHEN HE ARRIVED FOR THE SUMMIT.

Now arrange the circled letters to form the surprise answer, as suggested by the above cartoon.

Print answer here A "  "

JUMBLE®

Unscramble these four Jumbles, one letter to
each square, to form four ordinary words.

DEPTY

INJOT

SEATTL

RASTUX

We must
preserve its
history and
architecture

THE TALL BUILDING
WAS SAVED FROM
DEMOLITION BE-
CAUSE IT HAD A----

Now arrange the circled letters to form the
surprise answer, as suggested by the above
cartoon.

Print
answer
here   " ⬡⬡⬡⬡⬡⬡⬡ "   ⬡⬡⬡⬡

JUMBLE®

Unscramble these four Jumbles, one letter to each square, to form four ordinary words.

EUJIC

AGDEA

KUPPEE

CAPTEK

WHAT DAD LOOKED FORWARD TO WHEN JUNIOR FINISHED PIANO PRACTICE.

Now arrange the circled letters to form the surprise answer, as suggested by the above cartoon.

Print answer here

JUMBLE®

Unscramble these four Jumbles, one letter to each square, to form four ordinary words.

EUQUE

BOANT

SICCEN

FRAGEO

It's coming along nicely

WHAT A SCULPTOR DOES TO CREATE A STATUE FROM A STONE SLAB.

Now arrange the circled letters to form the surprise answer, as suggested by the above cartoon.

Print answer here " ☐☐☐☐☐☐☐ " IT ☐☐☐

JUMBLE®

Unscramble these four Jumbles, one letter to each square, to form four ordinary words.

NIXEV

GEMID

UNCIDE

BALIVE

This place looks seedy

BAR

WHETHER ON BOARD OR ON SHORE, A SUBMARINE CREW CAN BE----

Now arrange the circled letters to form the surprise answer, as suggested by the above cartoon.

Print answer here ⬡⬡ A " ⬡⬡⬡⬡ "

21

JUMBLE®

Unscramble these four Jumbles, one letter to
each square, to form four ordinary words.

YATTS

AKQUE

DAHLER

FLUITE

I'm going to
be making
twice as much
--BYE

WHEN THE MAID
GOT A BETTER
OFFER, THE
MATRON WAS----

Now arrange the circled letters to form the
surprise answer, as suggested by the above
cartoon.

*Print
answer
here*

IN THE " "

JUMBLE®

Unscramble these four Jumbles, one letter to each square, to form four ordinary words.

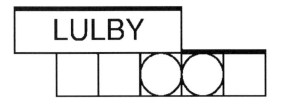

LULBY

DEBIA

NILUKE

WROFUR

ADULTS ONLY

X-RATED

HONKY TONK DANCERS

WHAT THE ZOO-KEEPER WAS ATTRACTED TO IN THE CITY.

Now arrange the circled letters to form the surprise answer, as suggested by the above cartoon.

Print answer here THE "

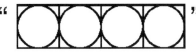

JUMBLE®

Unscramble these four Jumbles, one letter to
each square, to form four ordinary words.

NOWDY

IPSOE

ROCENE

HARXOT

Come take a
look. Only
$5 million

FOR
SALE

THE TYCOONS VIS-
ITED THE LUXURY
YACHT BECAUSE
IT WAS----

Now arrange the circled letters to form the
surprise answer, as suggested by the above
cartoon.

**Print answer
here** " ◯◯◯ "   ◯◯◯◯◯◯

JUMBLE®

Unscramble these four Jumbles, one letter to
each square, to form four ordinary words.

EWLEH

CINEE

ENVELE

DULSHO

WHOOEE!

Champagne
for everybody!

WHAT THE WILD-
CATTERS GOT
WHEN THEY HIT
A GUSHER.

Now arrange the circled letters to form the
surprise answer, as suggested by the above
cartoon.

*Print answer
here*

" "

JUMBLE®

Unscramble these four Jumbles, one letter to each square, to form four ordinary words.

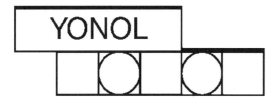

YONOL

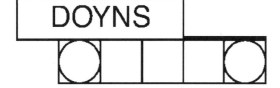

DOYNS

HEWEZE

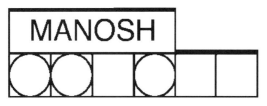

MANOSH

Who can tell me what this is?

YOU MIGHT SEE THIS IN A CLASSROOM.

Now arrange the circled letters to form the surprise answer, as suggested by the above cartoon.

Print answer here

A "◯◯◯◯" OF ◯◯◯◯◯

JUMBLE®

Getaway

Daily Puzzles

JUMBLE®

Unscramble these four Jumbles, one letter to each square, to form four ordinary words.

EVAUM

UPTYT

BERBOR

DAYDEL

STRIKE THREE!

I can't believe he struck out again

Can we listen to some music?

WHAT HE DID WHILE HE LISTENED TO THE BASEBALL GAME.

Now arrange the circled letters to form the surprise answer, as suggested by the above cartoon.

Print answer here ◯◯◯◯◯ HER " ◯◯◯◯◯ "

JUMBLE®

Unscramble these four Jumbles, one letter to
each square, to form four ordinary words.

INGOR

OAPIN

HURSTH

UNBOIN

Lend me
your ear

That's so
corny

A PLAY ON WORDS
CAN BE THIS.

Now arrange the circled letters to form the
surprise answer, as suggested by the above
cartoon.

Print answer " ◯◯◯ - ◯◯◯◯◯◯◯ "
here

JUMBLE®

Unscramble these four Jumbles, one letter to each square, to form four ordinary words.

REZIP

MYJUP

TEAQUE

TALBOC

Yikes! That's twice the estimate

WHAT THE ELEC-
TRICIAN GAVE THE
CUSTOMER WHEN HE
FINISHED THE JOB.

Now arrange the circled letters to form the surprise answer, as suggested by the above cartoon.

Print answer here ⬡⬡⬡⬡⬡ A " ⬡⬡⬡⬡ "

JUMBLE®

Unscramble these four Jumbles, one letter to
each square, to form four ordinary words.

FRUMO

GOROF

WODIMS

SNIPPE

If I lie down,
I'll fall asleep

THE TIRED CLIMBER
SAT ON THE
LEDGE BECAUSE
HE FEARED----

Now arrange the circled letters to form the
surprise answer, as suggested by the above
cartoon.

**Print
answer
here**   " ◯◯◯◯◯◯◯◯ " ◯◯◯◯

JUMBLE®

Unscramble these four Jumbles, one letter to each square, to form four ordinary words.

KELLN

HOOTT

CLUSIE

RELENK

That wins the match

18

PLOP!

WHEN THE ERRANT SHOT HIT THE GREEN, THE GOLFER SAID IT WAS----

Now arrange the circled letters to form the surprise answer, as suggested by the above cartoon.

Print answer here A " ◯◯◯◯◯◯ " OF ◯◯◯◯

JUMBLE®

Unscramble these four Jumbles, one letter to each square, to form four ordinary words.

GALED

WATEK

AURBUE

CUROHG

My knees are killing me

LAYING CARPETING CAN BE THIS.

Now arrange the circled letters to form the surprise answer, as suggested by the above cartoon.

Print answer here " ☐☐☐ - ☐☐☐ " ☐☐☐☐

JUMBLE®

Unscramble these four Jumbles, one letter to each square, to form four ordinary words.

RAAPK

TACCH

YIRAWA

DUNTIC

Ha-ha-ha

Hey! you tripped me!

WHAT THE SCHOOLYARD PRANK TURNED INTO WHEN HE END- ED UP IN THE MUD.

Now arrange the circled letters to form the surprise answer, as suggested by the above cartoon.

Print answer A here

" ◯◯◯◯◯ " ◯◯◯◯◯

JUMBLE®

Unscramble these four Jumbles, one letter to
each square, to form four ordinary words.

HASAW

NUMOD

NYLKID

CREFOD

Hiya, beautiful

HOW SHE FELT
WHEN THE MOBSTER
GAVE HER THE EYE.

Now arrange the circled letters to form the
surprise answer, as suggested by the above
cartoon.

**Print
answer
here**   "⬜⬜⬜⬜ - ⬜⬜⬜⬜⬜⬜"

JUMBLE®

Unscramble these four Jumbles, one letter to each square, to form four ordinary words.

SPUHL

USEAT

SMAJET

WURCEF

How many animals did that cost?

WHAT THE DIRECTOR SAID WHEN THE ACTRESS WORE THE EXPENSIVE FUR COAT.

Now arrange the circled letters to form the surprise answer, as suggested by the above cartoon.

Print answer here " ◯◯◯◯ ' ◯ A ◯◯◯◯◯ "

JUMBLE®

Unscramble these four Jumbles, one letter to each square, to form four ordinary words.

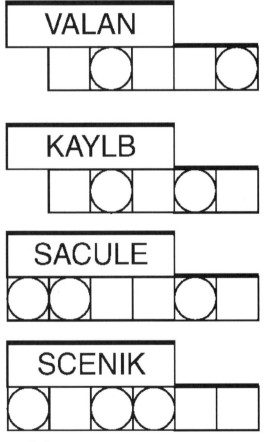

VALAN

KAYLB

SACULE

SCENIK

I'll take them in 4 inches at the waist

WHAT THE DIETER ENDED UP WITH WHEN HIS TROUSERS DIDN'T FIT.

Now arrange the circled letters to form the surprise answer, as suggested by the above cartoon.

Print answer A
here

JUMBLE®

Unscramble these four Jumbles, one letter to each square, to form four ordinary words.

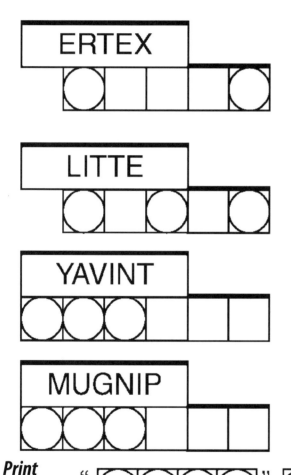

ERTEX

LITTE

YAVINT

MUGNIP

Nope, this isn't working

OUCH!

HOW HE DESCRIBED THE NEW NURSE'S EFFORT TO DRAW BLOOD.

Now arrange the circled letters to form the surprise answer, as suggested by the above cartoon.

Print answer A here

JUMBLE®

Unscramble these four Jumbles, one letter to
each square, to form four ordinary words.

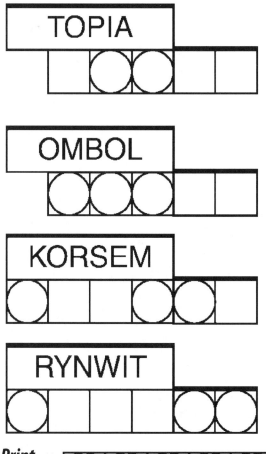

TOPIA

OMBOL

KORSEM

RYNWIT

It's hard,
and the
hours are
long

THE CIRCUS ANIMAL
TRAINER DESCRIBED
HIS JOB AS---

Now arrange the circled letters to form the
surprise answer, as suggested by the above
cartoon.

Print "◯◯◯◯◯◯◯" ◯◯◯◯
answer
here

39

JUMBLE®

Unscramble these four Jumbles, one letter to each square, to form four ordinary words.

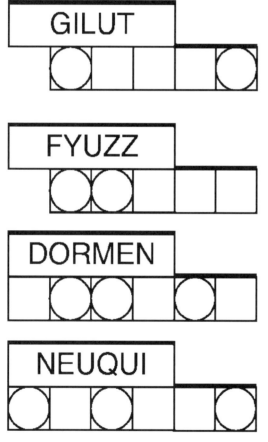

GILUT

FYUZZ

DORMEN

NEUQUI

All that for that?

HOW THE MATH WHIZ SOLVED THE COMPLEX PROBLEM.

Now arrange the circled letters to form the surprise answer, as suggested by the above cartoon.

Print answer here HE " ◯◯◯◯◯◯ " IT ◯◯◯

40

JUMBLE®

Unscramble these four Jumbles, one letter to each square, to form four ordinary words.

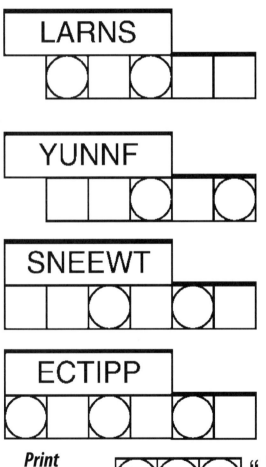

LARNS

YUNNF

SNEEWT

ECTIPP

Hi, Frank ol' pal

Sit down! Can't you see I'm busy?

WHY THE LOYAL CUSTOMER CHANGED BARBERS.

Now arrange the circled letters to form the surprise answer, as suggested by the above cartoon.

Print answer here HE  " "

JUMBLE®

Unscramble these four Jumbles, one letter to each square, to form four ordinary words.

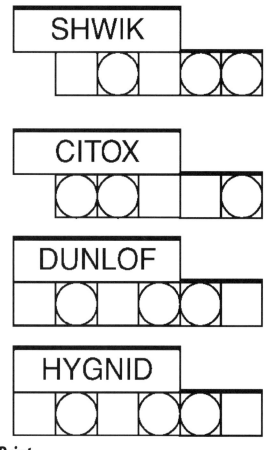

SHWIK

CITOX

DUNLOF

HYGNID

We've been rehearsing on the back lot for a week

AJAX FILM CO.

WHERE THE ACTORS TRAINED FOR THEIR ROLES AS MEDIEVAL WARRIORS.

Now arrange the circled letters to form the surprise answer, as suggested by the above cartoon.

Print answer AT here

"⃝⃝⃝⃝⃝⃝" ⃝⃝⃝⃝⃝⃝

JUMBLE®

Unscramble these four Jumbles, one letter to each square, to form four ordinary words.

BYDAN

DIXEO

SHABIN

ARRETH

Oh, my back! This pot is heavy

IN

WHAT THE CHEF EXPERIENCED WHEN HE POURED THE PASTA INTO THE COLANDER.

Now arrange the circled letters to form the surprise answer, as suggested by the above cartoon.

Print answer here A " ◯◯◯◯◯◯ "

JUMBLE®

Unscramble these four Jumbles, one letter to each square, to form four ordinary words.

LEJUP

VEREF

NECNAD

DUCADE

You will receive the going rate

WHAT SHE WAS PAID WHEN SHE BECAME A COVER GIRL.

Now arrange the circled letters to form the surprise answer, as suggested by the above cartoon.

Print answer here " ◯◯◯◯ " ◯◯◯◯◯

JUMBLE®

Unscramble these four Jumbles, one letter to each square, to form four ordinary words.

YURRC

RIFEA

REECLY

CEDBEK

Let's merge. We can cover twice as many events

Great idea

WHY THE RIVAL PHOTOGRAPHERS BECAME PARTNERS.

Now arrange the circled letters to form the surprise answer, as suggested by the above cartoon.

Print answer here THEY " ◯◯◯◯◯◯◯ "

JUMBLE®

Unscramble these four Jumbles, one letter to each square, to form four ordinary words.

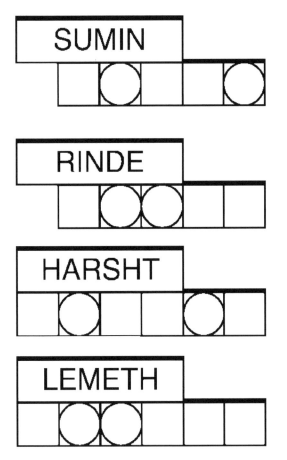

SUMIN

RINDE

HARSHT

LEMETH

SRO

Looks like a full house

WHAT THE COMEDIAN STUDIED BEFORE HIS ACT.

Now arrange the circled letters to form the surprise answer, as suggested by the above cartoon.

Print answer here  " "

JUMBLE®

Unscramble these four Jumbles, one letter to each square, to form four ordinary words.

CYDUH

HESOW

NITTAC

DILANI

Let's roast marsh-mallows

...and tell ghost stories

HOW MOM AND DAD MADE "LIGHT" OF IT WHEN THE POWER FAILED.

Now arrange the circled letters to form the surprise answer, as suggested by the above cartoon.

Print answer here

JUMBLE

Unscramble these four Jumbles, one letter to each square, to form four ordinary words.

PIMSK

TASHY

VEWERS

ENDOTE

Maybe she
won't come
back

WHEN THE STERN
TEACHER WENT ON
HER HONEYMOON,
SHE---

Now arrange the circled letters to form the surprise answer, as suggested by the above cartoon.

Print answer here

JUMBLE®

Unscramble these four Jumbles, one letter to each square, to form four ordinary words.

TIFAH

CIRLY

INGELT

NIFTEC

This wine goes well with your steak

Look! Real silverware

WHAT THE COUPLE ENJOYED WHEN THEY WERE UPGRADED TO FIRST CLASS.

Now arrange the circled letters to form the surprise answer, as suggested by the above cartoon.

Print answer here A ⬡⬡⬡⬡⬡⬡⬡ OF "⬡⬡⬡⬡⬡"

JUMBLE®

Unscramble these four Jumbles, one letter to
each square, to form four ordinary words.

BREEM

WOSOP

TEBICS

SARGIT

K.P. for everyone

He's nasty

WHY THE NEW
SERGEANT ACTED
LIKE A TIGER.

Now arrange the circled letters to form the
surprise answer, as suggested by the above
cartoon.

**Print
answer
here**   HE ◯◯◯ HIS " ◯◯◯◯◯◯◯ "

JUMBLE®

Unscramble these four Jumbles, one letter to each square, to form four ordinary words.

PLOIT

TASEC

SUMISE

HODRIC

I can cut it any way you like, thick, thin, butterflied

THIS WEEK'S SPECIAL

WHAT THE BUTCHER DID TO INCREASE SALES.

Now arrange the circled letters to form the surprise answer, as suggested by the above cartoon.

Print answer here " ◯◯◯◯◯◯ " ◯◯◯◯◯◯◯

JUMBLE®

Unscramble these four Jumbles, one letter to each square, to form four ordinary words.

LOPNY

WULFA

FAINAR

TARMIN

Right down the middle

He counts all his shots

WHAT THE GOLFER LIKED TO PLAY.

Now arrange the circled letters to form the surprise answer, as suggested by the above cartoon.

Print answer here THE " ☐☐☐☐☐ " ☐☐☐

JUMBLE®

Unscramble these four Jumbles, one letter to
each square, to form four ordinary words.

TAERF

YOWDD

REHIFE

BILDOY

Wedding Chapel

Now we
have to
tell our
families

WHAT THE YOUNG
LOVERS DID WHEN
THEY ELOPED.

Now arrange the circled letters to form the
surprise answer, as suggested by the above
cartoon.

Print answer here  TO

JUMBLE®

Unscramble these four Jumbles, one letter to each square, to form four ordinary words.

TIPEY

ARDOH

VIDDIE

MACENE

I'm tired of looking plain

Use eyeliner, too

WHEN SHE DECIDED TO IMPROVE HER LOOKS, SHE MADE UP---

Now arrange the circled letters to form the surprise answer, as suggested by the above cartoon.

Print answer here

JUMBLE®

Unscramble these four Jumbles, one letter to
each square, to form four ordinary words.

NEALK

MYPTE

ZEABAL

SNETEL

It's all to scale

What gauge
is the
track?

WHAT THE MINIA-
TURE RAILROAD
BUFFS INDULGED IN.

Now arrange the circled letters to form the
surprise answer, as suggested by the above
cartoon.

***Print answer
here*** "◯◯◯◯◯" ◯◯◯◯

JUMBLE®

Unscramble these four Jumbles, one letter to each square, to form four ordinary words.

ASOBS

PERIT

TURIAL

YAGELL

Relax, sailor. What's your problem?

WHEN HE REPORT-ED TO SICK BAY, HE WAS----

Now arrange the circled letters to form the surprise answer, as suggested by the above cartoon.

Print answer here

JUMBLE®

Unscramble these four Jumbles, one letter to each square, to form four ordinary words.

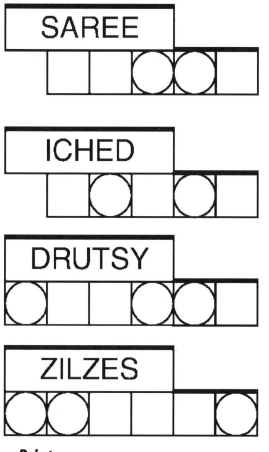

SAREE

ICHED

DRUTSY

ZILZES

...and here, on Pennsylvania Avenue...

A PRESIDENT WILL USE THE WHITE HOUSE FOR THIS.

Now arrange the circled letters to form the surprise answer, as suggested by the above cartoon.

Print answer here ◯◯◯ " ◯◯◯◯◯◯◯◯ "

JUMBLE®

Unscramble these four Jumbles, one letter to
each square, to form four ordinary words.

LOYKE

ORXYP

REBARN

ENTAIN

I told you not to use the
slingshot inside

WHEN THE LITTLE
PRINCE BROKE A
CASTLE WINDOW,
IT WAS A----

Now arrange the circled letters to form the
surprise answer, as suggested by the above
cartoon.

**Print answer
here**

JUMBLE®

Unscramble these four Jumbles, one letter to each square, to form four ordinary words.

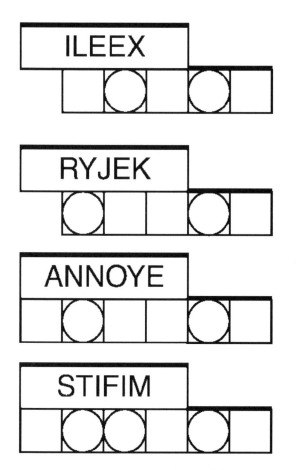

ILEEX

RYJEK

ANNOYE

STIFIM

The golf gods are against me

Just bad luck

THE GOLFER BLAMED THE MISS-ED PUTT ON A----

Now arrange the circled letters to form the surprise answer, as suggested by the above cartoon.

Print answer here

59

JUMBLE®

Unscramble these four Jumbles, one letter to each square, to form four ordinary words.

SINOE

PLIMB

DEECIV

PERSOC

That's outstanding

It's a good way to advertise

WHEN THE ARTIST GAVE HIMSELF A TATTOO, IT WAS----

Now arrange the circled letters to form the surprise answer, as suggested by the above cartoon.

Print answer here

"

"

60

JUMBLE®

Unscramble these four Jumbles, one letter to
each square, to form four ordinary words.

BUTOD

VILEA

DRENER

CAIFLE

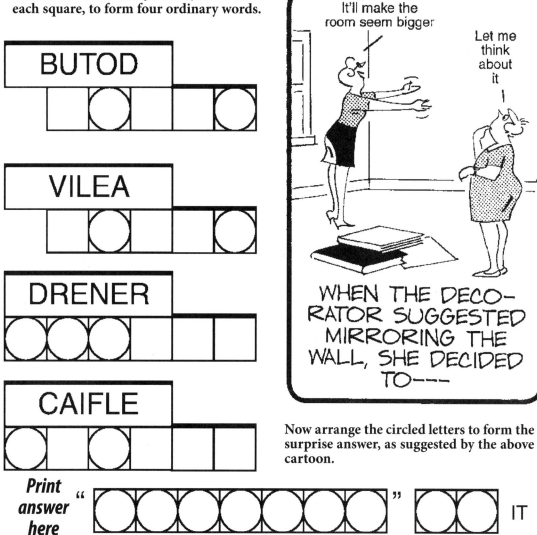

It'll make the
room seem bigger

Let me
think
about
it

WHEN THE DECO-
RATOR SUGGESTED
MIRRORING THE
WALL, SHE DECIDED
TO----

Now arrange the circled letters to form the
surprise answer, as suggested by the above
cartoon.

*Print
answer
here* " ◯◯◯◯◯◯◯ " ◯◯ IT

JUMBLE®

Unscramble these four Jumbles, one letter to each square, to form four ordinary words.

ARBSS

HELIT

MURIAD

LOPIET

This device is fast and easy

WHEN THE SALES-MAN DEMONSTRAT-ED TEXT MESSAG-ING, HE WAS----

Now arrange the circled letters to form the surprise answer, as suggested by the above cartoon.

Print answer here

JUMBLE®

Unscramble these four Jumbles, one letter to each square, to form four ordinary words.

PLEEO

HUGAL

TUGELL

NOOSAL

His honor outweighs him by 100 pounds

WHAT THE MAYOR USED TO WIN THE PICNIC TUG-OF-WAR.

Now arrange the circled letters to form the surprise answer, as suggested by the above cartoon.

Print answer here ◯◯◯◯ OF "◯◯◯◯"

JUMBLE®

Unscramble these four Jumbles, one letter to
each square, to form four ordinary words.

YITED

NEGIF

INVOIS

INBOAL

How's the
book, George?

It has more twists
than a mountain road

A GOOD MYSTERY IS
BOUND TO HAVE THIS.

Now arrange the circled letters to form the
surprise answer, as suggested by the above
cartoon.

*Print
answer* A
here

"   "

JUMBLE®

Unscramble these four Jumbles, one letter to each square, to form four ordinary words.

CEZAR

SHLYP

KOJECY

CUTLED

C'mon, Fred. It's time to go home

Too much to drink

WHAT THE OPTICIAN TURNED INTO AT THE PARTY.

Now arrange the circled letters to form the surprise answer, as suggested by the above cartoon.

Print answer here A " ⬡⬡⬡⬡⬡⬡⬡⬡⬡ "

JUMBLE®

Unscramble these four Jumbles, one letter to each square, to form four ordinary words.

PRIGE

ROCKA

DEIBES

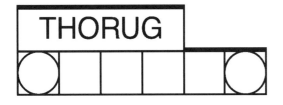

THORUG

Good soil, long growing season, Matilda. We'll do well

WHEN THE FARMER BOUGHT THE HUGE SPREAD, HE WAS----

Now arrange the circled letters to form the surprise answer, as suggested by the above cartoon.

Print answer here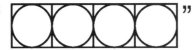

66

JUMBLE®

Unscramble these four Jumbles, one letter to each square, to form four ordinary words.

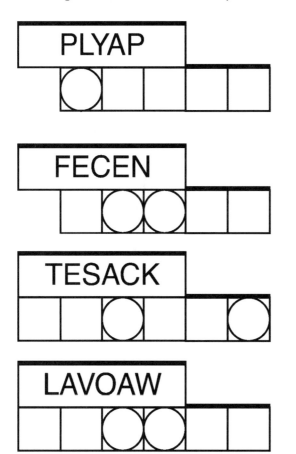

PLYAP

FECEN

TESACK

LAVOAW

It's ten degrees out there

I'll be fine

WHEN HE WENT FOR A WALK ON A COLD, WINDY DAY, IT WAS——

Now arrange the circled letters to form the surprise answer, as suggested by the above cartoon.

Print answer here ◯◯ " ◯◯◯◯◯ "

JUMBLE®

Unscramble these four Jumbles, one letter to each square, to form four ordinary words.

CREYM

GALOT

LOVEUM

CAFRIB

Thanks, Tommy

I've got to finish my route

WHERE THE PAPER BOY WENT WHEN HE RESCUED THE CAT.

Now arrange the circled letters to form the surprise answer, as suggested by the above cartoon.

Print answer here ◯◯◯ ON A ◯◯◯◯

JUMBLE®

Unscramble these four Jumbles, one letter to
each square, to form four ordinary words.

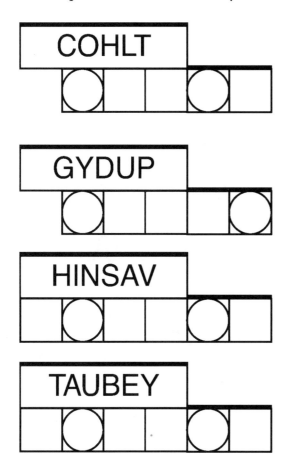

COHLT

GYDUP

HINSAV

TAUBEY

Why can't I
be the love
interest?

WHEN SHE PLAYED
THE ROLE OF A
SECRETARY, THE
STARLET WAS---

Now arrange the circled letters to form the
surprise answer, as suggested by the above
cartoon.

Print answer here " ◯◯◯◯ " ◯◯◯◯

JUMBLE®

Unscramble these four Jumbles, one letter to each square, to form four ordinary words.

VOIPT

KAHIK

CEADAR

LINGES

THE REVELERS SHUNNED THE TEETOTALER BECAUSE HE----

Now arrange the circled letters to form the surprise answer, as suggested by the above cartoon.

Print answer here

" "

JUMBLE®

Unscramble these four Jumbles, one letter to
each square, to form four ordinary words.

STEAE

ODTTI

REJUIN

SEECIX

You may kiss the bride

Oh, what
bliss

NO MATTER WHERE
IN THE WORLD,
MARRIAGES ALWAYS
BECOME---

Now arrange the circled letters to form the
surprise answer, as suggested by the above
cartoon.

Print
answer THE "◯◯◯◯◯◯" ◯◯◯◯◯◯
here

71

JUMBLE®

Unscramble these four Jumbles, one letter to each square, to form four ordinary words.

DONUP

RYTAR

DIPTUN

SCETOK

That's amazing

WHAT THE ECHO WAS TO THE BANKER.

Now arrange the circled letters to form the surprise answer, as suggested by the above cartoon.

Print answer here A " ⃝⃝⃝⃝⃝ " ⃝⃝⃝⃝⃝⃝

JUMBLE®

Unscramble these four Jumbles, one letter to
each square, to form four ordinary words.

REMIC

TRIGE

BASHUM

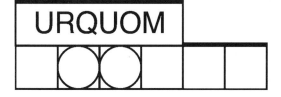

URQUOM

Those knots should
be gone

I feel
great

WHAT THE MOB
BOSS ALLOWED THE
MASSEUSE TO DO.

Now arrange the circled letters to form the
surprise answer, as suggested by the above
cartoon.

Print answer " ◯◯◯ " ◯◯◯ ◯◯◯
here

JUMBLE®

Unscramble these four Jumbles, one letter to each square, to form four ordinary words.

TARFD

BOLEN

TOOWWK

DYFLAG

We have a
two-week
special

OFFICE

Now we
can stay
longer

WHEN THE NATURE
CAMP CUT ITS RATE,
THE NUDISTS---

Now arrange the circled letters to form the surprise answer, as suggested by the above cartoon.

Print answer here

◯◯◯ **A** "◯◯◯" "◯◯◯"

JUMBLE®

Unscramble these four Jumbles, one letter to
each square, to form four ordinary words.

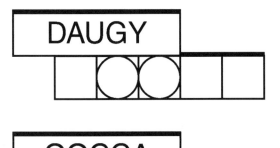

DAUGY

OOCCA

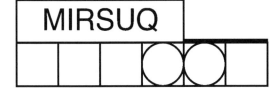

MIRSUQ

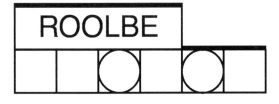

ROOLBE

More junk mail

Not worth opening

ALTHOUGH THE
MAILER WAS
OBLONG, THE
CONTENT WAS----

Now arrange the circled letters to form the
surprise answer, as suggested by the above
cartoon.

Print answer here "  "

75

JUMBLE®

Unscramble these four Jumbles, one letter to
each square, to form four ordinary words.

VORAB

ROODE

NECKAR

APITOE

Let's get
out of here

Give me
my robe

WHAT THE BEACH-
GOER DID WHEN THE
STORM APPROACHED.

Now arrange the circled letters to form the
surprise answer, as suggested by the above
cartoon.

*Print answer
here*

"   "

JUMBLE®

Unscramble these four Jumbles, one letter to each square, to form four ordinary words.

HOWSY

FOTIS

YALWEE

YUGLIT

Open all the windows

Can we get a hotel room?

WHAT THE FAMILY HAD TO DO UNTIL THE AIR CONDI- TIONER WAS FIXED.

Now arrange the circled letters to form the surprise answer, as suggested by the above cartoon.

Print answer here ⭘⭘⭘⭘⭘⭘ IT ⭘⭘⭘

JUMBLE®

Unscramble these four Jumbles, one letter to each square, to form four ordinary words.

GIMAC

CABIS

ENDECT

STENOX

There are lots of men

Tonight we'll go dancing

WHAT THE SINGLE WOMEN DID WHEN THEY TOOK A CRUISE.

Now arrange the circled letters to form the surprise answer, as suggested by the above cartoon.

Print answer here " ⬡⬡⬡⬡⬡ " THE ⬡⬡⬡⬡

JUMBLE®

Unscramble these four Jumbles, one letter to each square, to form four ordinary words.

ABOOT

BELAF

PYSEDE

KOOPHU

Longer hours, lower prices. Nothing works

OFTEN FOLLOWS WHEN A BUSINESS FALLS INTO THE RED.

Now arrange the circled letters to form the surprise answer, as suggested by the above cartoon.

Print answer here

JUMBLE®

Unscramble these four Jumbles, one letter to each square, to form four ordinary words.

SASEY

STUCO

NORBIN

LEWLOY

**%$#!!! You're 30 minutes behind

There goes my tip

WHAT THE SERVERS TURNED INTO WHEN THE KITCHEN WAS BACKED UP.

Now arrange the circled letters to form the surprise answer, as suggested by the above cartoon.

Print answer here " ◯◯◯◯◯◯◯ "

JUMBLE®

Unscramble these four Jumbles, one letter to
each square, to form four ordinary words.

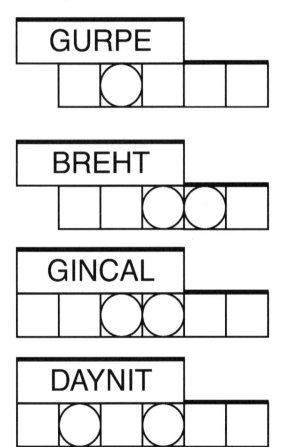

GURPE

BREHT

GINCAL

DAYNIT

What a
clown

KNOWN TO FALL
AT THE END OF A
PERFORMANCE.

Now arrange the circled letters to form the
surprise answer, as suggested by the above
cartoon.

Print answer here THE

JUMBLE®

Unscramble these four Jumbles, one letter to each square, to form four ordinary words.

NEARY

SIZEE

CROITE

EOPING

DIVORCE COURT

Ten lousy years, your honor

That's for sure

ALTHOUGH MARRIAGE IS JUST A WORD, IT CAN TURN INTO---

Now arrange the circled letters to form the surprise answer, as suggested by the above cartoon.

Print answer here A

JUMBLE®

Unscramble these four Jumbles, one letter to each square, to form four ordinary words.

JOBUM

LEBER

RIELOO

ELYSEP

I've got a headache and my stomach hurts

WHAT HE EXPERI-ENCED WHEN HE STUDIED MATH.

Now arrange the circled letters to form the surprise answer, as suggested by the above cartoon.

Print answer here " ⬡⬡⬡⬡⬡⬡⬡⬡ "

JUMBLE®

Unscramble these four Jumbles, one letter to each square, to form four ordinary words.

GENUB

NUCOE

GREJIG

GERBID

I thought this would be easy

Let's take a break

CLEANING A CARPET CAN BE A----

Now arrange the circled letters to form the surprise answer, as suggested by the above cartoon.

Print answer here " ◯◯◯◯◯◯ " ◯◯◯

JUMBLE®

Unscramble these four Jumbles, one letter to each square, to form four ordinary words.

ELVOH

RANOB

DREHWS

TARYEW

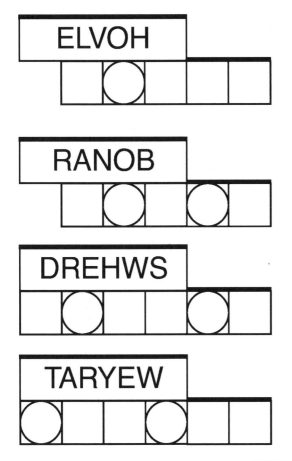

HALT! STOP!

Pull up the reins

WHAT THE TENDERFOOT EXPERIENCED ON HIS FIRST RIDE.

Now arrange the circled letters to form the surprise answer, as suggested by the above cartoon.

Print answer here A

JUMBLE®

Unscramble these four Jumbles, one letter to each square, to form four ordinary words.

KALEY

SYGGO

CEEDDO

RATVAC

THE DIFFERENCE
BETWEEN A CANARY
AND A CAT.

Now arrange the circled letters to form the surprise answer, as suggested by the above cartoon.

Print answer here ⬡⬡⬡⬡⬡ AND ⬡⬡⬡⬡⬡

JUMBLE®

Unscramble these four Jumbles, one letter to each square, to form four ordinary words.

RANGL

POOTH

ENNOIT

REFOBE

Not a bad day's work

WHAT THE FISHER-MAN WAS LEFT WITH WHEN HE SOLD HIS CATCH.

Print answer A *here*

" "

Now arrange the circled letters to form the surprise answer, as suggested by the above cartoon.

JUMBLE®

Unscramble these four Jumbles, one letter to each square, to form four ordinary words.

THAPC

CRIHB

RUSHOC

SAWLAY

I'm looking forward to intense discussions

WHEN THE PRO-FESSORS TOOK A CRUISE, THE OCEAN LINER BECAME A----

Now arrange the circled letters to form the surprise answer, as suggested by the above cartoon.

Print answer here

JUMBLE®

Unscramble these four Jumbles, one letter to
each square, to form four ordinary words.

GIREM

NOMEW

NIDIOE

YARTTE

It's
too
big

It just
needs
pruning

WHAT THE LARGE
CHRISTMAS TREE
NEEDED.

Now arrange the circled letters to form the
surprise answer, as suggested by the above
cartoon.

Print answer here " "

JUMBLE®

Unscramble these four Jumbles, one letter to each square, to form four ordinary words.

WETTE

MUHID

VOONCY

SYVURC

He's always looking downfield

WHEN THE STAR QUARTERBACK LEARNED TO FLY, HE WAS GOOD AT----

Now arrange the circled letters to form the surprise answer, as suggested by the above cartoon.

Print answer here

JUMBLE®

Unscramble these four Jumbles, one letter to each square, to form four ordinary words.

STOUJ

ALVIA

REMAID

FAHBLE

You call this
a haircut?

WHAT THE RECRUIT
DID WHEN THE ARMY
BARBER FINISHED.

Now arrange the circled letters to form the surprise answer, as suggested by the above cartoon.

Print answer here HE " "

JUMBLE®

Unscramble these four Jumbles, one letter to each square, to form four ordinary words.

NIGVY

NOCIT

HAMFOT

BERROK

**%$#!!! It won't turn over

WHAT HAPPENED WHEN THE OLD-TIMER COULDN'T START HIS CAR.

Now arrange the circled letters to form the surprise answer, as suggested by the above cartoon.

Print answer here HE " "

JUMBLE®

Unscramble these four Jumbles, one letter to each square, to form four ordinary words.

LEWJE

LUFOR

MAIROH

FLOWEL

WHEN MOM SAW
THE TODDLER'S ART-
WORK, SHE WAS----

Now arrange the circled letters to form the surprise answer, as suggested by the above cartoon.

Print answer here " ☐☐☐ THE ☐☐☐☐ "

JUMBLE®

Unscramble these four Jumbles, one letter to each square, to form four ordinary words.

HOTBO

SERCS

SAROUE

NORREC

Make sure the
helmet is
tight

WHAT THE TEACHER
TOOK BEFORE HE
ENTERED THE
DEMOLITION RACE.

Now arrange the circled letters to form the
surprise answer, as suggested by the above
cartoon.

*Print
answer* A
here

" ⃝⃝⃝⃝⃝ " ⃝⃝⃝⃝⃝⃝

JUMBLE®

Unscramble these four Jumbles, one letter to each square, to form four ordinary words.

FEWRA

ROIVS

YENLOP

EXVONC

That's the way. Nice job

IMPORTANT TO DO FOR A YOUNG COWBOY.

Now arrange the circled letters to form the surprise answer, as suggested by the above cartoon.

Print answer here

[ ] [ ] [ ] [ ] [ ] THE " [ ] [ ] [ ] [ ] [ ] "

JUMBLE®

Unscramble these four Jumbles, one letter to
each square, to form four ordinary words.

NEECH

YUINF

GUDDIE

CORRET

Everyone will
know Jane's
name

WHEN SHE MARRIED
THE FAMOUS CELE-
BRITY, SHE WAS----

Now arrange the circled letters to form the
surprise answer, as suggested by the above
cartoon.

**Print answer
here** " ◯◯ - ◯◯◯◯◯◯◯ "

96

JUMBLE®

Unscramble these four Jumbles, one letter to each square, to form four ordinary words.

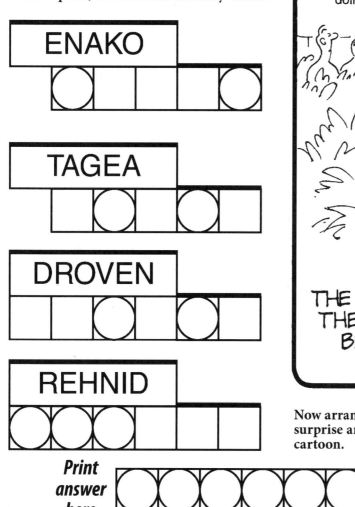

ENAKO

TAGEA

DROVEN

REHNID

We didn't have anything doing this weekend

NUDIST COLONY

THE COUPLE VISITED THE NATURE CAMP BECAUSE THEY HAD---

Now arrange the circled letters to form the surprise answer, as suggested by the above cartoon.

Print answer here

" "

JUMBLE®

Unscramble these four Jumbles, one letter to each square, to form four ordinary words.

HILEW

ESING

HAXLEE

YARRET

They're so in love

THIS CAN LEAD TO THE ALTAR

Now arrange the circled letters to form the surprise answer, as suggested by the above cartoon.

Print answer here

JUMBLE®

Unscramble these four Jumbles, one letter to each square, to form four ordinary words.

HINEW

DROLE

TIPPEC

ASTUNE

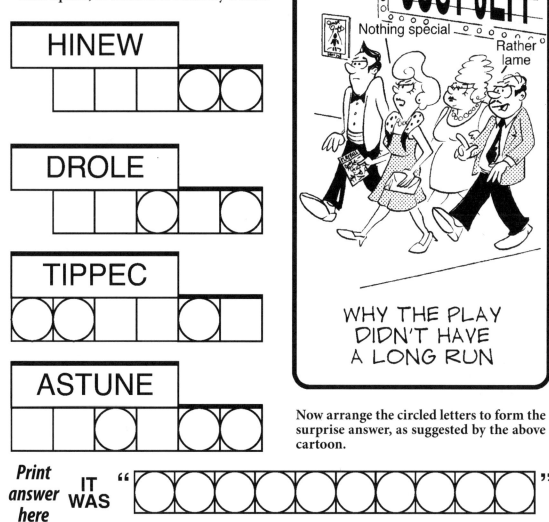

JUST JEFF

Nothing special

Rather lame

WHY THE PLAY DIDN'T HAVE A LONG RUN

Now arrange the circled letters to form the surprise answer, as suggested by the above cartoon.

Print answer here

IT WAS "⟨ ⟩"

JUMBLE®

Unscramble these four Jumbles, one letter to each square, to form four ordinary words.

SCOUF

RASCY

RULBET

WEDDEG

Meet the new vice president

CRANE & SON LLC

WHAT YOU CAN DO AT FIRST, IF YOU'RE THE BOSS' SON

Now arrange the circled letters to form the surprise answer, as suggested by the above cartoon.

Print answer here

JUMBLE®

Unscramble these four Jumbles, one letter to each square, to form four ordinary words.

ADYLL

UNPER

NIJYET

YUBILS

What have I done?

MOST BRIDES LOOK STUNNING, BUT SOME GROOMS ARE ---

Now arrange the circled letters to form the surprise answer, as suggested by the above cartoon.

Print answer here

JUMBLE®

Unscramble these four Jumbles, one letter to each square, to form four ordinary words.

EXIDO

NUMIS

WHENEP

FALOTA

Just salad and lean meat

THE CROSS-COUNTRY TRUCKER STAYED THIN WHEN HE WATCHED THIS ---

Now arrange the circled letters to form the surprise answer, as suggested by the above cartoon.

Print answer here THE " ◯◯◯◯ " ◯◯◯◯◯◯

JUMBLE®

Unscramble these four Jumbles, one letter to
each square, to form four ordinary words.

KWATE

REHKI

MAUTER

NODARP

I'm so
embarrassed

WHEN THE WEALTHY
MATRON WAS
CAUGHT SHOPLIFTING,
SHE FOUND IT ---

Now arrange the circled letters to form the
surprise answer, as suggested by the above
cartoon.

**Print
answer
here**

"

"

103

JUMBLE®

Unscramble these four Jumbles, one letter to each square, to form four ordinary words.

KIMPS

VOYNE

YULOHN

CLUBEK

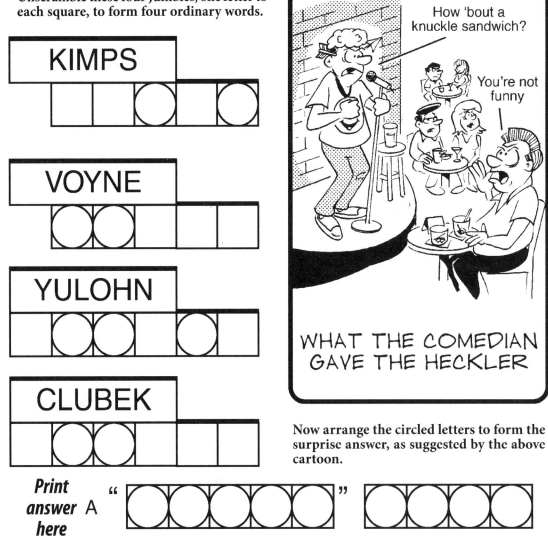

How 'bout a knuckle sandwich?

You're not funny

WHAT THE COMEDIAN GAVE THE HECKLER

Now arrange the circled letters to form the surprise answer, as suggested by the above cartoon.

Print answer here A " ⬡⬡⬡⬡⬡ " ⬡⬡⬡⬡

JUMBLE®

Unscramble these four Jumbles, one letter to each square, to form four ordinary words.

MALFE

NULAN

TOMSED

HEERCY

How's the family?

THIS HELPS
CONSTRUCTION
WORKERS BOND

Now arrange the circled letters to form the surprise answer, as suggested by the above cartoon.

Print answer here

105

JUMBLE®

Unscramble these four Jumbles, one letter to each square, to form four ordinary words.

HIRMT

PARPE

RUVESS

ANIZIN

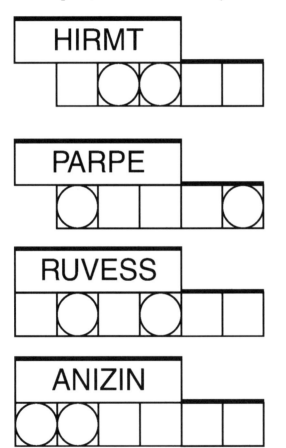

...and the winner is...

Well I'll be...

WHEN HE WON THE DISTINGUISHED GENTLEMAN CONTEST, IT WAS A - - -

Now arrange the circled letters to form the surprise answer, as suggested by the above cartoon.

Print answer here

JUMBLE®

Unscramble these four Jumbles, one letter to each square, to form four ordinary words.

YOOST

TYKIT

FLOUND

CHROID

WE PUMP!

5.9
UNLEA

BOTH GASOLINE
AND ELECTRICITY
CAN DO THIS

Now arrange the circled letters to form the surprise answer, as suggested by the above cartoon.

Print answer here " ◯◯◯◯◯ " ◯◯◯

JUMBLE®

Unscramble these four Jumbles, one letter to
each square, to form four ordinary words.

RUYLS

YEMSS

INCOVE

THARRE

What's that strong
fragrance?

Smells cheap

WHAT THE SHOPPERS
TURNED UP AT THE
PERFUME COUNTER

Now arrange the circled letters to form the
surprise answer, as suggested by the above
cartoon.

**Print answer
here**

JUMBLE®

Unscramble these four Jumbles, one letter to
each square, to form four ordinary words.

SIGUE

NORST

DAWTOR

THEESE

Daddy, this is
a scary story

MANY AUTHORS
OF HALLOWEEN
BOOKS ARE ----

Now arrange the circled letters to form the
surprise answer, as suggested by the above
cartoon.

*Print
answer
here* " ⬡⬡⬡⬡⬡ " ⬡⬡⬡⬡⬡⬡⬡⬡

JUMBLE®

Unscramble these four Jumbles, one letter to
each square, to form four ordinary words.

MAXIO

NOARP

NUGMIP

QUESMO

TEST TOMORROW

Not again

WHAT SHE IS IN AN
ENGLISH CLASS?

Now arrange the circled letters to form the
surprise answer, as suggested by the above
cartoon.

Print answer here A

JUMBLE®

Unscramble these four Jumbles, one letter to
each square, to form four ordinary words.

ROFAL

DORAH

LESUNS

MEHRIT

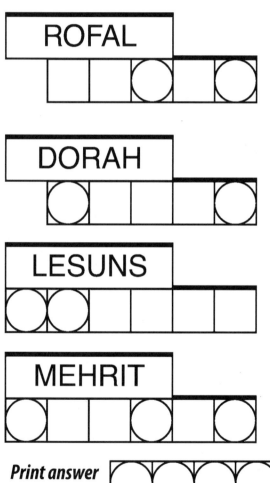

Can you believe
the cost of gas?

FOR A DENTIST,
MAKING A
LIVING IS ---

Now arrange the circled letters to form the
surprise answer, as suggested by the above
cartoon.

*Print answer
here* TO

JUMBLE®

Unscramble these four Jumbles, one letter to each square, to form four ordinary words.

REESA

TELIT

ETTORP

GUMPSY

UNWRAPPING THEIR TREATS DURING THE COWBOY MOVIE MADE THEM ---

Now arrange the circled letters to form the surprise answer, as suggested by the above cartoon.

Print answer here

JUMBLE®

Unscramble these four Jumbles, one letter to
each square, to form four ordinary words.

FRADT

SAYES

TYLLAF

MISTEK

I only buy on
sale and use coupons

A GOOD WAY TO
MAKE MONEY LAST.

Now arrange the circled letters to form the
surprise answer, as suggested by the above
cartoon.

Print answer here 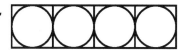 IT

JUMBLE®

Unscramble these four Jumbles, one letter to
each square, to form four ordinary words.

GOTEB

RUFIT

PREDON

JUINER

Let's see.
If I hit this key,
then...

WHAT THE SALES
CLERK DID WHEN HE
FIRST USED A
CALCULATOR.

Now arrange the circled letters to form the
surprise answer, as suggested by the above
cartoon.

Print
answer
here   " ◯◯◯◯◯◯◯ " IT ◯◯◯

114

JUMBLE®

Unscramble these four Jumbles, one letter to
each square, to form four ordinary words.

FLAIN

ENVIL

MULVLE

MOINCE

As long as I'm
with you

Are you okay?

WHEN THE
SWEETHEARTS
SLIPPED ON THE ICE,
THEY---

Now arrange the circled letters to form the
surprise answer, as suggested by the above
cartoon.

*Print
answer
here*

115

JUMBLE®

Unscramble these four Jumbles, one letter to each square, to form four ordinary words.

REDOO

OAQUT

UNGLIB

GLABEM

He's joining the symphony orchestra

WILCO

THE PIANO PLAYER QUIT THE POP BAND BECAUSE HE WANTED TO ---

Now arrange the circled letters to form the surprise answer, as suggested by the above cartoon.

Print answer here ◯◯◯ FOR ◯◯◯◯◯◯◯

JUMBLE®

Unscramble these four Jumbles, one letter to each square, to form four ordinary words.

SCABI

CHOAR

WHERDS

TUSALE

Next

I itch all over

Me too

THIS CAN KEEP A SKIN DOCTOR BUSY.

Now arrange the circled letters to form the surprise answer, as suggested by the above cartoon.

Print answer here A ⬡⬡⬡⬡ OF ⬡⬡⬡⬡⬡⬡

JUMBLE®

Unscramble these four Jumbles, one letter to each square, to form four ordinary words.

VENIA

TALEE

LACCIO

LUNYUR

They are starting to look shaggy

I can make you a good deal

STAGE MANAGER

WHEN THE DRAPERY SALESMAN VISITED THE THEATER, IT WAS A ---

Now arrange the circled letters to form the surprise answer, as suggested by the above cartoon.

Print answer here

JUMBLE®

Unscramble these four Jumbles, one letter to
each square, to form four ordinary words.

TINAF

HAGUL

LYNFOD

RETHOX

I love your hair

Watch your back
around her

A REPUTATION AS
TWO-FACED
MADE HER ---

Now arrange the circled letters to form the
surprise answer, as suggested by the above
cartoon.

*Print
answer
here*   ◯◯◯◯◯◯◯ OR " ◯◯◯◯ "

119

JUMBLE®

Unscramble these four Jumbles, one letter to each square, to form four ordinary words.

LUDEE

LIMPE

WEDOMA

VAHLED

Perfect. I must have them for the party

WHEN SHE BOUGHT THE EXPENSIVE PARTY SHOES, SHE WAS ----

Now arrange the circled letters to form the surprise answer, as suggested by the above cartoon.

Print answer here

JUMBLE®

Unscramble these four Jumbles, one letter to each square, to form four ordinary words.

BLAWR

KNARC

BUCHYB

AHVEBE

THIS CAN KEEP ASTRONAUTS ON THE GROUND.

Now arrange the circled letters to form the surprise answer, as suggested by the above cartoon.

Print answer A
here

JUMBLE®

Unscramble these four Jumbles, one letter to each square, to form four ordinary words.

INCCY

DOLYD

DEGAMA

DARCCO

Don't upset him

shhh

HOW TO KEEP A RHINO FROM CHARGING.

Now arrange the circled letters to form the surprise answer, as suggested by the above cartoon.

Print answer here

HIS

JUMBLE®

Unscramble these four Jumbles, one letter to each square, to form four ordinary words.

UDGIE

IMREC

CITILE

UMRAIB

See you at the reception

WHAT THE BRIDE AND GROOM HAD AT THEIR WEDDING.

Now arrange the circled letters to form the surprise answer, as suggested by the above cartoon.

Print answer here A "⬭⬭⬭⬭" ⬭⬭⬭⬭

JUMBLE®

Unscramble these four Jumbles, one letter to each square, to form four ordinary words.

KUYDS

RACZE

FIURAN

INTOUG

Watch out for that car

Why don't you take the wheel?

WHAT A BACK SEAT DRIVER SELDOM SEEMS TO DO.

Now arrange the circled letters to form the surprise answer, as suggested by the above cartoon.

Print answer here ☐☐☐ ☐☐☐ OF " ☐☐☐ "

JUMBLE®

Unscramble these four Jumbles, one letter to each square, to form four ordinary words.

TIDEY

RECSS

LOMOGY

RUNUTE

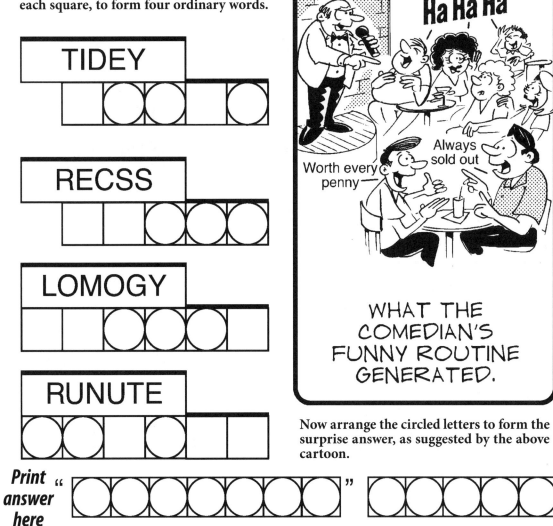

Ha Ha Ha

Worth every penny

Always sold out

WHAT THE COMEDIAN'S FUNNY ROUTINE GENERATED.

Now arrange the circled letters to form the surprise answer, as suggested by the above cartoon.

Print answer here " ⬡⬡⬡⬡⬡⬡⬡ " ⬡⬡⬡⬡⬡

JUMBLE®

Unscramble these four Jumbles, one letter to each square, to form four ordinary words.

VOYCE

NUWDE

BOALIN

LISWEY

Can you believe she's getting divorced again?

WHEN THE HIGHER UPS APPEAR IN GOSSIP COLUMNS, READERS OFTEN GET THE – – –

Now arrange the circled letters to form the surprise answer, as suggested by the above cartoon.

Print answer here

126

JUMBLE®

Unscramble these four Jumbles, one letter to
each square, to form four ordinary words.

FYNAC

ACCOO

MEEDAF

GIRFID

I cook all our meals.
Never order out

IT'S EASIER TO STICK
TO A DIET THESE
DAYS IF YOU
EAT WHAT YOU ---

Now arrange the circled letters to form the
surprise answer, as suggested by the above
cartoon.

*Print answer
here*

JUMBLE®

Unscramble these four Jumbles, one letter to each square, to form four ordinary words.

PRIVE

DEEKY

DROWPE

WHADOS

THE HOSTS MADE
THE VISITORS FEEL
AT HOME
WHEN THEY ---

Now arrange the circled letters to form the surprise answer, as suggested by the above cartoon.

Print answer here

 THEY

JUMBLE®

Unscramble these four Jumbles, one letter to each square, to form four ordinary words.

CREMY

SURVI

EEFELC

TEXENT

Phew! Let's get out of here

WHEN THE SKUNK DREW THE CROWD'S ATTENTION, IT BECAME THE ---

Now arrange the circled letters to form the surprise answer, as suggested by the above cartoon.

Print answer here " ⃝⃝⃝⃝⃝⃝⃝ " OF IT

JUMBLE®

Unscramble these four Jumbles, one letter to each square, to form four ordinary words.

SYMSO

WETET

LEENED

WEABER

I could get used to this

Sure beats slinging hash

WHAT THE WAITERS TURNED INTO ON VACATION.

Now arrange the circled letters to form the surprise answer, as suggested by the above cartoon.

Print answer here

JUMBLE®

Unscramble these four Jumbles, one letter to each square, to form four ordinary words.

KLIMY

NADDY

BEJOCT

SYPEDE

WHEN THEY EXCHANGED WORDS IN THE SAUNA, THINGS GOT --

Now arrange the circled letters to form the surprise answer, as suggested by the above cartoon.

Print answer here " ◯◯◯◯◯◯ "

JUMBLE®

Unscramble these four Jumbles, one letter to each square, to form four ordinary words.

MASCH

RAMEK

SHUCOR

UPTYDE

You're through

Ooops! Missed

TOO MANY BEERS ON THE JOB LEFT THE CARPENTER – – –

Now arrange the circled letters to form the surprise answer, as suggested by the above cartoon.

Print answer here " ◯◯◯◯◯◯◯◯ "

132

JUMBLE®

Unscramble these four Jumbles, one letter to each square, to form four ordinary words.

YUSHK

LOBOD

TEPICK

BIUMED

Wait! I overslept

WHAT THE FISHERMAN DID WHEN HIS HELPER WAS LATE.

Now arrange the circled letters to form the surprise answer, as suggested by the above cartoon.

Print answer "⃝⃝⃝⃝⃝⃝" ⃝⃝⃝
here

JUMBLE®

Unscramble these four Jumbles, one letter to each square, to form four ordinary words.

METHY

MONGE

MESORK

SEWBOT

Whatever you
want, my dear

HOW HE FELT WHEN
HIS WIFE BOUGHT
A BIG DIAMOND.

Now arrange the circled letters to form the surprise answer, as suggested by the above cartoon.

Print answer here " ⬯⬯⬯⬯⬯ " ⬯⬯⬯⬯⬯

JUMBLE®

Unscramble these four Jumbles, one letter to each square, to form four ordinary words.

CHURS

EUSAP

GURTED

FLOUBE

Hurry, you're falling behind

LAP 48

WHAT THE BIKE RACER FELT WHEN HE FIXED THE FLAT TIRE.

Now arrange the circled letters to form the surprise answer, as suggested by the above cartoon.

Print answer here " ⃝⃝⃝⃝⃝⃝⃝⃝ "

JUMBLE®

Unscramble these four Jumbles, one letter to
each square, to form four ordinary words.

DEGEH

ESSOU

YEMBOR

YALSAW

It will go right through town

This is
complicated

WHAT IT TAKES TO
UNVEIL PLANS FOR
A NEW HIGHWAY.

Now arrange the circled letters to form the
surprise answer, as suggested by the above
cartoon.

**Print answer
here** A "  "

JUMBLE®

Unscramble these four Jumbles, one letter to each square, to form four ordinary words.

CHABT

BIELL

THRUNE

NEEGIN

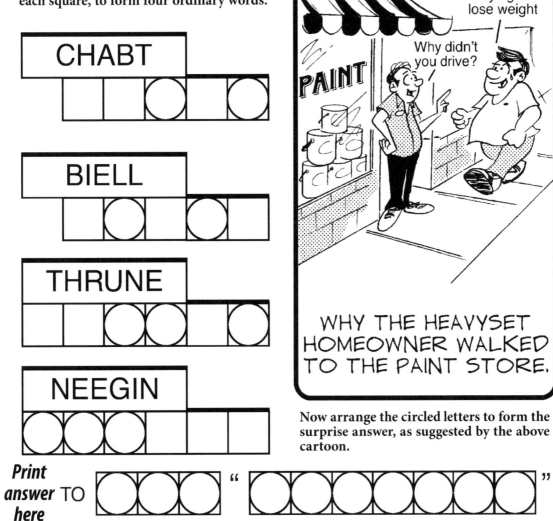

PAINT

Why didn't you drive?

Trying to lose weight

WHY THE HEAVYSET HOMEOWNER WALKED TO THE PAINT STORE.

Now arrange the circled letters to form the surprise answer, as suggested by the above cartoon.

Print answer TO *here*

"   "

JUMBLE®

Unscramble these four Jumbles, one letter to each square, to form four ordinary words.

WOPOH

KANLY

CORHUG

NECBOK

WHEN THE SHEPHERDS WENT FISHING, THEY WORKED BY ---

Now arrange the circled letters to form the surprise answer, as suggested by the above cartoon.

Print answer here

[ ] [ ] [ ] [ ] [ ] OR [ ] [ ] [ ] [ ] [ ] [ ] [ ] [ ]

JUMBLE®

Unscramble these four Jumbles, one letter to
each square, to form four ordinary words.

ORPEN

ANGLD

WAIBLE

STIGED

I'll fix you up

WHAT THE HOCKEY
TEAM'S DENTIST DID
WHEN THE PLAYER
LOST SOME TEETH.

Now arrange the circled letters to form the
surprise answer, as suggested by the above
cartoon.

**Print
answer
here** " ⭕⭕⭕⭕⭕⭕⭕ " THE ⭕⭕⭕

JUMBLE®

Unscramble these four Jumbles, one letter to
each square, to form four ordinary words.

PHECO

PIPNY

SMIDOW

DUMEGS

A double
chocolate cone

AFTER THE BOXER
LOST THE FIGHT,
HE LICKED --

Now arrange the circled letters to form the
surprise answer, as suggested by the above
cartoon.

*Print answer
here*

JUMBLE®

Unscramble these four Jumbles, one letter to each square, to form four ordinary words.

SUMIC

ROBAR

COLLEA

TECKOP

Let's go talk to the judge

WHAT THE SHOP-LIFTER FACED WHEN HE TOOK THE BEST-SELLER.

Now arrange the circled letters to form the surprise answer, as suggested by the above cartoon.

Print answer here A ⬡⬡⬡⬡⬡ " ⬡⬡⬡⬡⬡ "

JUMBLE®

Unscramble these four Jumbles, one letter to each square, to form four ordinary words.

USVEA

SILAA

JEGLIG

TEXCIE

All clear to surface

WHEN THE CAPTAIN RAISED THE PERISCOPE, THE SUBMARINE WAS AT ---

Now arrange the circled letters to form the surprise answer, as suggested by the above cartoon.

Print answer here " ◯◯◯ " ◯◯◯◯◯

JUMBLE®

Unscramble these four Jumbles, one letter to each square, to form four ordinary words.

ROFOL

SOUME

SARGYS

HYSTAN

WHAT THE OVER-
WORKED
SONGSTRESS
SUFFERED

Now arrange the circled letters to form the surprise answer, as suggested by the above cartoon.

Print answer here

143

JUMBLE®

Unscramble these four Jumbles, one letter to
each square, to form four ordinary words.

TOFUL

TENFO

NEAFED

TIVEHR

It's Mrs. Smith

Take a number

MOM DIDN'T ANSWER
THE PHONE BECAUSE
SHE WAS ---

Now arrange the circled letters to form the
surprise answer, as suggested by the above
cartoon.

*Print
answer
here* ◯◯ ◯◯◯ " ◯◯◯◯ "

JUMBLE®

Unscramble these four Jumbles, one letter to each square, to form four ordinary words.

MYLAD

RYFIA

RICKYT

GLUFEN

He never hurries

Works in slow motion

WHAT THE SCULPTOR WAS KNOWN FOR.

Now arrange the circled letters to form the surprise answer, as suggested by the above cartoon.

Print answer here HIS 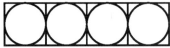 OF

JUMBLE®

Unscramble these four Jumbles, one letter to each square, to form four ordinary words.

NOMUT

RAMEF

CEITED

BLOGIE

I'll put her on the cover

She's worth top dollar

A MODEL WITH A NICE FIGURE CAN GET THIS.

Now arrange the circled letters to form the surprise answer, as suggested by the above cartoon.

Print answer here A ⬭⬭⬭⬭ ⬭⬭⬭⬭⬭⬭⬭

JUMBLE®

Unscramble these four Jumbles, one letter to
each square, to form four ordinary words.

KOAWE

ALLAM

PARMEC

GRIINF

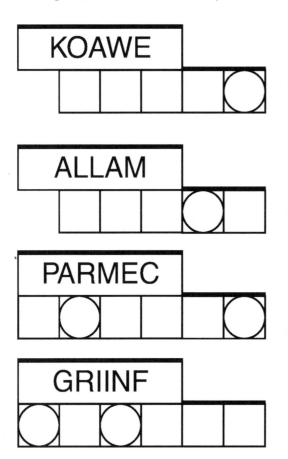

Hoed all the rows, boss.
What's next?

WHAT THE HIRED
HAND CULTIVATED
TO GET AHEAD.

Now arrange the circled letters to form the
surprise answer, as suggested by the above
cartoon.

Print answer here   THE

JUMBLE®

Unscramble these four Jumbles, one letter to each square, to form four ordinary words.

JAROM

TANCH

FRUTOH

CURPES

You're my first patient

I itch all over

WHEN THE SKIN DOCTOR OPENED HIS PRACTICE, HE STARTED ---

Now arrange the circled letters to form the surprise answer, as suggested by the above cartoon.

Print answer here

" "

JUMBLE®

Unscramble these four Jumbles, one letter to
each square, to form four ordinary words.

SEBOE

CHULG

LAJIED

BLUSTY

Don't forget your garter

WHAT THE BRIDE
DID AT THE MAKEUP
TABLE

Now arrange the circled letters to form the
surprise answer, as suggested by the above
cartoon.

Print answer here SHE " ◯◯◯◯◯◯◯ "

JUMBLE.

Unscramble these four Jumbles, one letter to
each square, to form four ordinary words.

DIPEW

YURLT

BEFLAD

NAHRGE

I was here first!

No you weren't!

HANG IN THERE

WHAT HAPPENED WHEN
BOTH EMPLOYEES
WANTED THE LAST
CUP OF COFFEE.

Now arrange the circled letters to form the
surprise answer, as suggested by the above
cartoon.

**Print
answer
here** A ⬡⬡⬡⬡⬡ " ⬡⬡⬡⬡⬡⬡ "

JUMBLE®

Unscramble these four Jumbles, one letter to each square, to form four ordinary words.

CRAHN

MAGLE

CATLEK

SIBUHL

But it's the middle of the game

WHEN THE SPORTS FAN'S BIG-SCREEN TV WAS REPOSSESSED, HE SUFFERED ---

Now arrange the circled letters to form the surprise answer, as suggested by the above cartoon.

Print answer here A " ◯◯◯ ◯◯◯◯ "

JUMBLE®

Unscramble these four Jumbles, one letter to each square, to form four ordinary words.

DUXEE

WICTE

ENGOUT

BRENZA

Check your mouthpiece and tank

ALL LESSONS 50% OFF

WHAT THE DIVING INSTRUCTOR DID TO KEEP HIS BUSINESS AFLOAT.

Now arrange the circled letters to form the surprise answer, as suggested by the above cartoon.

Print answer here

" "

JUMBLE®

Unscramble these four Jumbles, one letter to each square, to form four ordinary words.

KIREP

SHECS

LADVAN

RITHEH

Everybody buckle up

WHY HE INSISTED THAT HIS FAMILY WEAR SEAT BELTS.

Now arrange the circled letters to form the surprise answer, as suggested by the above cartoon.

Print answer TO *here*

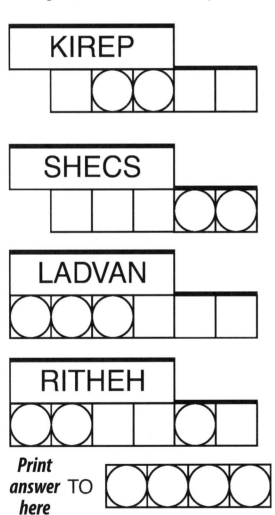

JUMBLE®

Unscramble these four Jumbles, one letter to
each square, to form four ordinary words.

DAULT

OMIDI

CHINTS

THOGTE

It's a perfectly
fine meal.
EAT UP!

SHE WASN'T A GOOD
COOK, BUT SHE WAS
GOOD AT THIS.

Now arrange the circled letters to form the
surprise answer, as suggested by the above
cartoon.

*Print
answer
here*

" ⭕⭕⭕⭕⭕⭕⭕ " IT ⭕⭕⭕

JUMBLE®

Unscramble these four Jumbles, one letter to
each square, to form four ordinary words.

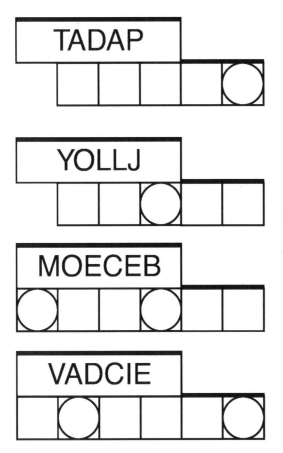

TADAP

YOLLJ

MOECEB

VADCIE

It's just firecrackers

POP! POP! POP!

Quick, out the back!

WHAT THE LOCK-
SMITH DID WHEN HE
THOUGHT HE HEARD
GUNFIRE.

Now arrange the circled letters to form the
surprise answer, as suggested by the above
cartoon.

Print answer here HE " ⃝⃝⃝⃝⃝⃝ "

JUMBLE®

Unscramble these four Jumbles, one letter to each square, to form four ordinary words.

DEGIM

CONTH

TINNEY

UNPOWT

How 'bout dinner and a movie?

It's dinner OR a movie

IN THESE TIMES OF TIGHT BUDGETS, STAYING WITHIN MEANS----

Now arrange the circled letters to form the surprise answer, as suggested by the above cartoon.

Print answer here

JUMBLE®

Unscramble these four Jumbles, one letter to each square, to form four ordinary words.

KILSY

PHRAC

LARROP

FRAMOT

Not again

ALTHOUGH SKIING IS POPULAR IN WINTERTIME, IT CAN BE A ---

Now arrange the circled letters to form the surprise answer, as suggested by the above cartoon.

Print answer here A " ◯◯◯◯ " ◯◯◯◯◯◯

JUMBLE

Unscramble these four Jumbles, one letter to
each square, to form four ordinary words.

ALMEY

UPOHC

TREETH

TAIREW

When will you
be back?

Later, Mom

WHAT JUNIOR
ANSWERED WHEN
MOM ASKED HOW
LONG HE'D BE GONE.

Now arrange the circled letters to form the
surprise answer, as suggested by the above
cartoon.

**Print answer
here** THE

JUMBLE®

Unscramble these four Jumbles, one letter to each square, to form four ordinary words.

GANTY

VOYIR

GRAFEO

BILBEN

Try the third drawer

HIS SECRETARY WAS GOOD AT THIS.

Now arrange the circled letters to form the surprise answer, as suggested by the above cartoon.

Print answer here " ◯◯◯◯◯◯ "

JUMBLE®

Unscramble these four Jumbles, one letter to each square, to form four ordinary words.

YURST

THAWE

SUSTLY

WARROH

This is awful. Take it back

HOW THE GERMAN DINER DESCRIBED HIS MEAL.

Now arrange the circled letters to form the surprise answer, as suggested by the above cartoon.

Print answer here THE ◯◯◯◯◯ ◯◯◯◯◯

160

JUMBLE®

Unscramble these four Jumbles, one letter to
each square, to form four ordinary words.

YOSIN

TAVIL

FLEMUF

BLOTTE

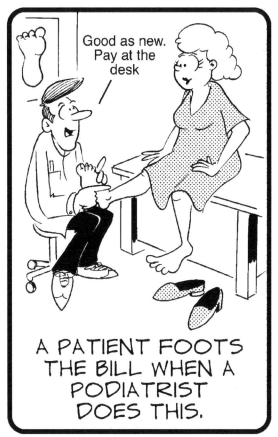

Good as new.
Pay at the
desk

A PATIENT FOOTS
THE BILL WHEN A
PODIATRIST
DOES THIS.

Now arrange the circled letters to form the
surprise answer, as suggested by the above
cartoon.

*Print
answer
here*

THE

JUMBLE®

Unscramble these four Jumbles, one letter to each square, to form four ordinary words.

CLAWR

HAFFC

POWALL

CUSENS

Sounds good. Put $20 on him to win

WHAT THE VET MADE AT THE RACETRACK.

Now arrange the circled letters to form the surprise answer, as suggested by the above cartoon.

Print answer here

" ☐☐☐☐☐ " ☐☐☐☐☐

JUMBLE Getaway

Challenger Puzzles

JUMBLE®

Unscramble these six Jumbles, one letter to each square, to form six ordinary words.

MOURUQ

CRUDEE

WAHGIE

CLAGEY

NAHVIS

BIMGAT

#$&!!!★★
MORE delays!

CLOSED FOR REPAIRS
ALL TRAFFIC

WHY THE STREET
WORKERS PUT UP
DETOUR SIGNS.

Now arrange the circled letters to form the surprise answer, as suggested by the above cartoon.

Print answer here

TO ◯◯◯◯ ◯◯◯◯◯ "◯◯◯◯"

JUMBLE®

Unscramble these six Jumbles, one letter to each square, to form six ordinary words.

PONISH

INCLAG

TACIOM

ZELPUZ

SPECHY

FOISSY

There! Now I can see myself better

WHY THE CELEBRITY BAD BOY DECIDED TO CLEAN THE MIRROR.

Now arrange the circled letters to form the surprise answer, as suggested by the above cartoon.

Print answer here

TO ◯◯◯◯◯◯ ◯◯◯ ◯◯◯◯◯

JUMBLE®

Unscramble these six Jumbles, one letter to
each square, to form six ordinary words.

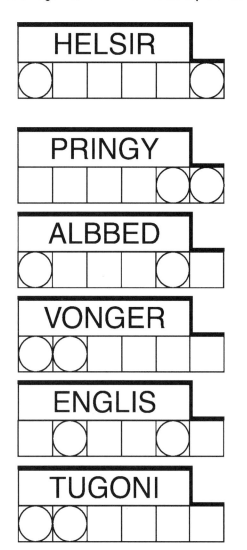

HELSIR

PRINGY

ALBBED

VONGER

ENGLIS

TUGONI

I can't
keep up

I'll take
two dozen

WHEN THE BAKER'S
CREATIONS WERE A
SMASH HIT, HE
WAS——

Now arrange the circled letters to form the
surprise answer, as suggested by the above
cartoon.

Print answer here

" ⬭⬭⬭⬭⬭⬭⬭ " **IN** ⬭⬭⬭⬭⬭

JUMBLE®

Unscramble these six Jumbles, one letter to each square, to form six ordinary words.

FRUIGE

BLUBEA

TEABED

SWANER

BLAMME

DEVACI

He's making eight different meals at once

ON A BUSY NIGHT, THE VERSATILE CHEF PREPARED A——

Now arrange the circled letters to form the surprise answer, as suggested by the above cartoon.

Print answer here

◯◯◯◯◯ " ◯◯◯◯◯◯ " OF ◯◯◯◯◯◯

167

JUMBLE®

Unscramble these six Jumbles, one letter to each square, to form six ordinary words.

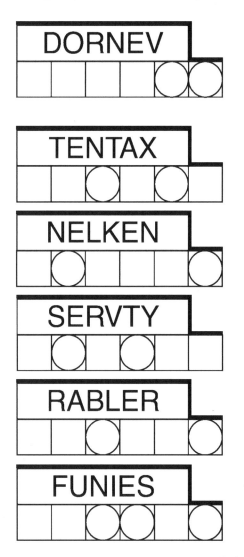

DORNEV

TENTAX

NELKEN

SERVTY

RABLER

FUNIES

...and to my son, William, I leave five million dollars

WHAT THE ATTORNEY TURNED INTO WHEN HE READ THE WILL.

Now arrange the circled letters to form the surprise answer, as suggested by the above cartoon.

Print answer here

A " ⃝⃝⃝⃝⃝⃝ " ⃝⃝⃝⃝⃝⃝

JUMBLE

Unscramble these six Jumbles, one letter to each square, to form six ordinary words.

INMERV

CHEWEN

LAWASY

GILBOE

CLAISO

GLARBE

This 9 to 5 stuff is driving me nuts

HOW THE MOUN-
TAINEER WHO TOOK
AN OFFICE JOB
ENDED UP.

Now arrange the circled letters to form the surprise answer, as suggested by the above cartoon.

Print answer here

JUMBLE®

Unscramble these six Jumbles, one letter to
each square, to form six ordinary words.

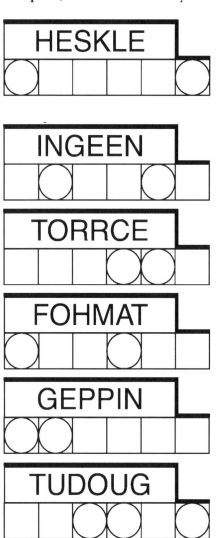

HESKLE

INGEEN

TORRCE

FOHMAT

GEPPIN

TUDOUG

It's the fastest
way to the gate

WHEN THE PASSEN-
GERS TOOK THE
AIRPORT STAIRS, IT
WAS A———

Now arrange the circled letters to form the
surprise answer, as suggested by the above
cartoon.

Print answer here

JUMBLE®

Unscramble these six Jumbles, one letter to each square, to form six ordinary words.

EUMMUS

MAANSE

GUBBED

DOITUS

RONACE

SHAREE

Not bad

Needs salt

You'll get better

WHAT THE YOUNG COOK NEEDED TO SUCCEED.

Now arrange the circled letters to form the surprise answer, as suggested by the above cartoon.

Print answer here

" "

171

JUMBLE®

Unscramble these six Jumbles, one letter to
each square, to form six ordinary words.

COTESK

FACSIO

LANNID

YACKEL

RYBBAC

SOWDRY

Don't share this
technique with
anyone

THE BAKER
REVEALED HIS TOP
SECRET RECIPE
ON A---

Now arrange the circled letters to form the
surprise answer, as suggested by the above
cartoon.

Print answer here

" ⬡⬡⬡⬡⬡⬡ " TO ⬡⬡⬡⬡⬡ ⬡⬡⬡⬡⬡⬡

JUMBLE®

Unscramble these six Jumbles, one letter to each square, to form six ordinary words.

TELRUT

PEESLY

BORREK

YESWIL

TREBUT

BANACA

It's held together by glue and wire

WHAT THE MUSEUM USED TO ASSEMBLE THE DINOSAUR BONES.

Now arrange the circled letters to form the surprise answer, as suggested by the above cartoon.

Print answer here

A " ⬡⬡⬡⬡⬡⬡⬡⬡ " ⬡⬡⬡⬡

JUMBLE®

Unscramble these six Jumbles, one letter to each square, to form six ordinary words.

LEWOLF

THYROW

YALMIN

YESWIL

DORIAT

ZIEFER

We're almost there

Fifty miles without water

WHEN THE DESERT TREKKERS SAW THE OASIS, IT WAS----

Now arrange the circled letters to form the surprise answer, as suggested by the above cartoon.

Print answer here

" ⃝⃝⃝⃝ " **ON** ⃝⃝⃝⃝⃝ ⃝⃝⃝

JUMBLE®

Unscramble these six Jumbles, one letter to each square, to form six ordinary words.

YAHMME

DEBBIA

BRUCHE

BONBBI

EMSIDE

GUMSED

You forgot your coat

WHAT THE OBNOXIOUS PARTY-GOER LEFT.

Now arrange the circled letters to form the surprise answer, as suggested by the above cartoon.

Print answer here

TO

JUMBLE®

Unscramble these six Jumbles, one letter to
each square, to form six ordinary words.

TULYSS

STACOM

FLORAM

TOYBUN

YIRRAT

BOIDUT

Pay attention
to your
homework

I
am

STARGAZING CAN
BE GOOD WHEN
YOU DO THIS.

Now arrange the circled letters to form the
surprise answer, as suggested by the above
cartoon.

Print answer here

176

JUMBLE®

Unscramble these six Jumbles, one letter to
each square, to form six ordinary words.

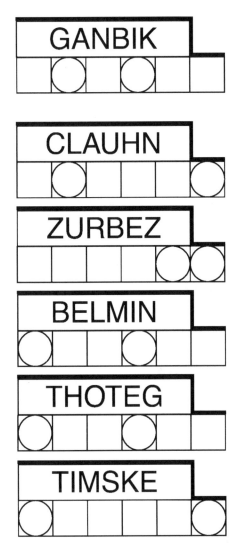

GANBIK

CLAUHN

ZURBEZ

BELMIN

THOTEG

TIMSKE

It's gorgeous

It's
a
little
tight

Are
those
real
diamonds?

WEARING A
CHOKER CAN BE----

Now arrange the circled letters to form the
surprise answer, as suggested by the above
cartoon.

Print answer here

177

JUMBLE®

Unscramble these six Jumbles, one letter to
each square, to form six ordinary words.

OLDBOY

INSLUM

PLATEA

TOALZE

LARIAD

RORTER

...and it only costs $750,000

Have you got anything in a nice runabout?

WHAT IT TOOK
TO BUY THE YACHT.

Now arrange the circled letters to form the
surprise answer, as suggested by the above
cartoon.

Print answer here

A ⬭⬭⬭⬭⬭⬭⬭⬭ OF ⬭⬭⬭⬭⬭

JUMBLE®

Unscramble these six Jumbles, one letter to
each square, to form six ordinary words.

PRYSAT

GINDAR

EMBLUH

THINCS

GINFIX

THENUR

We've always wanted
to do this

THEY TOOK A
MOUNTAIN VACATION
BECAUSE IT WAS----

Now arrange the circled letters to form the
surprise answer, as suggested by the above
cartoon.

Print answer here

"⬡⬡⬡⬡" ON ⬡⬡⬡⬡⬡ ⬡⬡⬡⬡

JUMBLE®

Unscramble these six Jumbles, one letter to each square, to form six ordinary words.

ROCFAT

TUGIRA

YUPRIF

ETOLAC

COORTH

EXYONG

How many?

THE BOXER
TURNED CENSUS
TAKER WAS---

Now arrange the circled letters to form the surprise answer, as suggested by the above cartoon.

Print answer here

◯◯◯ ◯◯◯ ◯◯◯ " ◯◯◯◯◯◯ "

JUMBLE®

Unscramble these six Jumbles, one letter to each square, to form six ordinary words.

BOUGER

TALMED

ZELZUG

CENTEM

LOOGGI

HINCUR

YOU'RE ALL WET, YOUR HONOR

You are close to contempt, counselor

WHAT THE LAWYER DID WHEN HE HOLLERED AT THE JUDGE.

Now arrange the circled letters to form the surprise answer, as suggested by the above cartoon.

Print answer here

"◯◯◯◯◯◯◯" ◯◯◯◯◯◯◯◯

JUMBLE®

Unscramble these six Jumbles, one letter to
each square, to form six ordinary words.

YAMBIG

TANFIN

YIVERF

GREENE

EECCAD

THANYS

SHE ALWAYS WORE
THIS OUTFIT IN
THE HUNT BECAUSE
IT WAS HER---

Now arrange the circled letters to form the
surprise answer, as suggested by the above
cartoon.

Print answer here

" "

182

JUMBLE®

Unscramble these six Jumbles, one letter to each square, to form six ordinary words.

REVINT

TORETT

BALEEG

RAFIAS

SNUFIO

OMIERM

You know you still owe me $200

I do?

SOMETIMES DEVEL-
OPED WHEN YOU
BORROW MONEY.

Now arrange the circled letters to form the surprise answer, as suggested by the above cartoon.

Print answer here

183

Answers

1. **Jumbles:** CLOVE CRANK MIDDAY FUMBLE
   Answer: How the mechanic described the coffee—"BREAK" FLUID

2. **Jumbles:** SKUNK DRAWL WOBBLE BOTTLE
   Answer: What happened to the library thief?—HE WAS "BOOKED"

3. **Jumbles:** PEONY ALTAR ITALIC BEWAIL
   Answer: Not telling the truth can be—A LIE-ABILITY

4. **Jumbles:** TEMPO VALET CASHEW PLENTY
   Answer: What the shoplifter got when he took the fancy calendar—TWELVE MONTHS

5. **Jumbles:** DICED TRULY OUTFIT POLISH
   Answer: When she helped Mom bake a cake, she turned into a—"FLOUR" CHILD

6. **Jumbles:** BIPED GULCH SUBMIT TURNIP
   Answer: What the former artist did when he returned to the easel—"BRUSHED" UP

7. **Jumbles:** CREEL TRACT FLORID DISMAY
   Answer: Where the tour group went to view the sea mammals—THE "OTTER" SIDE

8. **Jumbles:** GUILE OCTET TRUANT DELUGE
   Answer: What the captain gave the new helmsman—"LATITUDE"

9. **Jumbles:** QUOTA CHESS SECEDE DUPLEX
   Answer: When the pumpkin was weighed, the record was—"SQUASHED"

10. **Jumbles:** MOLDY OFTEN INNING CUDGEL
    Answer: What the ship's captain did when he got a computer—"LOGGED" ON

11. **Jumbles:** UNCAP BLANK ADJOIN TINKLE
    Answer: The novice duck hunters attributed their success to—"BLIND" LUCK

12. **Jumbles:** ANNOY GAWKY FEUDAL BEFALL
    Answer: His day off turned into this when he woke up with a cold—AN OFF DAY

13. **Jumbles:** DECRY GAVEL INDIGO OUTLAW
    Answer: After years of study, the portly scholar was—WELL "ROUNDED"

14. **Jumbles:** BEFOG ADMIT KILLER INDOOR
    Answer: What the sugar daddy did when she shopped for shoes—"FOOTED" THE BILL

15. **Jumbles:** CROUP BLESS CHISEL SQUALL
    Answer: Worn by the rowing team for the big race—"SCULL" CAPS

16. **Jumbles:** TWICE GAMUT CRAYON SPRUCE
    Answer: The statesman was given this when he arrived for the summit—A "REPORT"

17. **Jumbles:** TYPED JOINT LATEST SURTAX
    Answer: The tall building was saved from demolition because it had a—"STORIED" PAST

18. **Jumbles:** JUICE ADAGE UPKEEP PACKET
    Answer: What Dad looked forward to when Junior finished piano practice—PIECE PEACE

19. **Jumbles:** QUEUE BATON SCENIC FORAGE
    Answer: What a sculptor does to create a statue from a stone slab—"FIGURES" IT OUT

20. **Jumbles:** VIXEN MIDGE INDUCE VIABLE
    Answer: Whether on board or on shore, a submarine crew can be—IN A "DIVE"

21. **Jumbles:** TASTY QUAKE HERALD FUTILE
    Answer: When the maid got a better offer, the matron was—LEFT IN THE "DUST"

22. **Jumbles:** BULLY ABIDE UNLIKE FURROW
    Answer: What the zookeeper was attracted to in the city—THE "WILD" LIFE

23. **Jumbles:** DOWNY POISE ENCORE THORAX
    Answer: The tycoons visited the luxury yacht because it was—"SEE"WORTHY

24. **Jumbles:** WHEEL NIECE ELEVEN SHOULD
    Answer: What the wildcatters got when they hit a gusher—WELL "OILED"

25. **Jumbles:** LOONY SYNOD WHEEZE HANSOM
    Answer: You might see this in a classroom—A "SHOW" OF HANDS

26. **Jumbles:** MAUVE PUTTY ROBBER DEADLY
    Answer: What he did while he listened to the baseball game—DROVE HER "BATTY"

27. **Jumbles:** GROIN PIANO THRUSH BUNION
    Answer: A play on words can be this—"PUN-ISHING"

28. **Jumbles:** PRIZE JUMPY EQUATE COBALT
    Answer: What the electrician gave the customer when he finished the job—QUITE A "JOLT"

29. **Jumbles:** FORUM FORGO WISDOM PEPSIN
    Answer: The tired climber sat on the ledge because he feared—"DROPPING" OFF

30. **Jumbles:** KNELL TOOTH SLUICE KERNEL
    Answer: When the errant shot hit the green, the golfer said it was—A "STROKE" OF LUCK

31. **Jumbles:** GLADE TWEAK BUREAU GROUCH
    Answer: Laying carpeting can be this—"RUG-GED"WORK

32. **Jumbles:** PARKA CATCH AIRWAY INDUCT
    Answer: What the schoolyard prank turned into when he ended up in the mud—A "DIRTY" TRICK

33. **Jumbles:** AWASH MOUND KINDLY FORCED
    Answer: How she felt when the mobster gave her the eye—"HOOD-WINKED"

34. **Jumbles:** PLUSH SAUTE JETSAM CURFEW
    Answer: What the director said when the actress wore the expensive fur coat—"THAT'S A WRAP"

35. **Jumbles:** NAVAL BALKY CLAUSE SICKEN
    Answer: What the dieter ended up with when his trousers didn't fit—A SLACK SLACK

36. **Jumbles:** EXERT TITLE VANITY IMPUGN
    Answer: How he described the new nurse's effort to draw blood—A "VEIN" ATTEMPT

37. **Jumbles:** PATIO BLOOM SMOKER WINTRY
    Answer: The circus animal trainer described his job as—"BEASTLY"WORK

38. **Jumbles:** GUILT FUZZY MODERN UNIQUE
    Answer: How the math whiz solved the complex problem—HE "FIGURED" IT OUT

39. **Jumbles:** SNARL FUNNY NEWEST PEPTIC
    Answer: Why the loyal customer changed barbers—HE WAS "SNIPPY"

40. **Jumbles:** WHISK TOXIC UNFOLD DINGHY
    Answer: Where the actors trained for their roles as medieval warriors—AT "KNIGHT" SCHOOL

41. **Jumbles:** BANDY OXIDE BANISH RATHER
    Answer: What the chef experienced when he poured the pasta into the colander—A "STRAIN"

42. **Jumbles:** JULEP FEVER CANNED ADDUCE
    Answer: What she was paid when she became a cover girl—"FACE" VALUE

43. **Jumbles:** CURRY AFIRE CELERY BEDECK
    Answer: Why the rival photographers became partners—THEY "CLICKED"

44. **Jumbles:** MINUS DINER THRASH HELMET
    Answer: What the comedian studied before his act—HIS "LINES"

45. **Jumbles:** DUCHY WHOSE INTACT INLAID
    Answer: How Mom and Dad made "light" of it when the power failed—WITH CANDLES

46. **Jumbles:** SKIMP HASTY SWERVE DENOTE
    Answer: When the stern teacher went on her honeymoon, she—WASN'T "MISSED"

47. **Jumbles:** FAITH LYRIC TINGLE INFECT
Answer: What the couple enjoyed when they were upgraded to first class—A FLIGHT OF "FANCY"

48. **Jumbles:** EMBER SWOOP BISECT GRATIS
Answer: Why the new sergeant acted like a tiger—HE GOT HIS "STRIPES"

49. **Jumbles:** PILOT CASTE MISUSE ORCHID
Answer: What the butcher did to increase sales—"SLICED" PRICES

50. **Jumbles:** PYLON AWFUL FARINA MARTIN
Answer: What the golfer liked to play—THE "FAIR" WAY

51. **Jumbles:** AFTER DOWDY HEIFER BODILY
Answer: What the young lovers did when they eloped—FLED TO WED

52. **Jumbles:** PIETY HOARD DIVIDE MENACE
Answer: When she decided to improve her looks, she made up—HER MIND

53. **Jumbles:** ANKLE EMPTY ABLAZE NESTLE
Answer: What the miniature railroad buffs indulged in—"SMALL" TALK

54. **Jumbles:** BASSO TRIPE RITUAL GALLEY
Answer: When he reported to sick bay, he was—ILL, AT EASE

55. **Jumbles:** ERASE CHIDE STURDY SIZZLE
Answer: A President will use the White House for this—HIS "ADDRESS"

56. **Jumbles:** YOKEL PROXY BARREN INNATE
Answer: When the little prince broke a castle window, it was a—ROYAL "PANE"

57. **Jumbles:** EXILE JERKY ANYONE MISFIT
Answer: The golfer blamed the missed putt on a—LINKS JINX

58. **Jumbles:** NOISE BLIMP DEVICE CORPSE
Answer: When the artist gave himself a tattoo, it was—"IMPRESSIVE"

59. **Jumbles:** DOUBT ALIVE RENDER FACILE
Answer: When the decorator suggested mirroring the wall, she decided to—"REFLECT" ON IT

60. **Jumbles:** BRASS LITHE RADIUM POLITE
Answer: When the salesman demonstrated text messaging, he was—ALL THUMBS

61. **Jumbles:** ELOPE LAUGH GULLET SALOON
Answer: What the Mayor used to win the picnic tug-of-war—LOTS OF PULL

62. **Jumbles:** DEITY FEIGN VISION ALBINO
Answer: A good mystery is bound to have this—A "NOVEL" ENDING

63. **Jumbles:** CRAZE SYLPH JOCKEY DULCET
Answer: What the optician turned into at the party—A "SPECTACLE"

64. **Jumbles:** GRIPE CROAK BESIDE TROUGH
Answer: When the farmer bought the huge spread, he was—"DIRT" RICH

65. **Jumbles:** APPLY FENCE CASKET AVOWAL
Answer: When he went for a walk on a cold, windy day, it was—NO "SWEAT"

66. **Jumbles:** MERCY GLOAT VOLUME FABRIC
Answer: Where the paper boy went when he rescued the cat—OUT ON A LIMB

67. **Jumbles:** CLOTH PUDGY VANISH BEAUTY
Answer: When she played the role of a secretary, the starlet was—"TYPE" CAST

68. **Jumbles:** PIVOT KHAKI ARCADE SINGLE
Answer: The revelers shunned the teetotaler because he—LACKED "SPIRIT"

69. **Jumbles:** TEASE DITTO INJURE EXCISE
Answer: No matter where in the world, marriages always become—THE "UNITED" STATES

70. **Jumbles:** POUND TARRY PUNDIT SOCKET
Answer: What the echo was to the banker—A "SOUND" RETURN

71. **Jumbles:** CRIME TIGER AMBUSH QUORUM
Answer: What the mob boss allowed the masseuse to do—"RUB" HIM OUT

72. **Jumbles:** DRAFT NOBLE KOWTOW GADFLY
Answer: When the nature camp cut its rate, the nudists—GOT A LOT "OFF"

73. **Jumbles:** GAUDY COCOA SQUIRM BOLERO
Answer: Although the mailer was oblong, the content was—"CIRCULAR"

74. **Jumbles:** BRAVO RODEO CANKER OPIATE
Answer: What the beachgoer did when the storm approached—TOOK "COVER"

75. **Jumbles:** SHOWY FOIST LEEWAY GUILTY
Answer: What the family had to do until the air conditioner was fixed—SWEAT IT OUT

76. **Jumbles:** MAGIC BASIC DECENT SEXTON
Answer: What the single women did when they took a cruise—"MISSED" THE BOAT

77. **Jumbles:** TABOO FABLE SPEEDY HOOKUP
Answer: Often follows when a business falls into the red—THE BLUES

78. **Jumbles:** ESSAY SCOUT INBORN YELLOW
Answer: What the servers turned into when the kitchen was backed up—"WAITERS"

79. **Jumbles:** PURGE BERTH LACING DAINTY
Answer: Known to fall at the end of a performance—THE CURTAIN

80. **Jumbles:** YEARN SEIZE EROTIC PIGEON
Answer: Although marriage is just a word, it can turn into—A SENTENCE

81. **Jumbles:** JUMBO REBEL ORIOLE SLEEPY
Answer: What he experienced when he studied math—"PROBLEMS"

82. **Jumbles:** BEGUN OUNCE JIGGER BRIDGE
Answer: Cleaning a carpet can be a—"RUGGED" JOB

83. **Jumbles:** HOVEL BARON SHREWD WATERY
Answer: What the tenderfoot experienced on his first ride—A WHOA WOE

84. **Jumbles:** LEAKY SOGGY DECODE CRAVAT
Answer: The difference between a canary and a cat—CAGED AND CAGEY

85. **Jumbles:** GNARL PHOTO INTONE BEFORE
Answer: What the fisherman was left with when he sold his catch—A "NET" PROFIT

86. **Jumbles:** PATCH BIRCH CHORUS ALWAYS
Answer: When the professors took a cruise, the ocean liner became a—SCHOLAR SHIP

87. **Jumbles:** GRIME WOMEN IODINE TREATY
Answer: What the large Christmas tree needed—"TRIMMING"

88. **Jumbles:** TWEET HUMID CONVOY SCURVY
Answer: When the star quarterback learned to fly, he was good at—TOUCHDOWNS

89. **Jumbles:** JOUST AVAIL ADMIRE BEHALF
Answer: What the recruit did when the Army barber finished—HE "BRISTLED"

90. **Jumbles:** VYING TONIC FATHOM BROKER
Answer: What happened when the old-timer couldn't start his car—HE GOT "CRANKY"

91. **Jumbles:** JEWEL FLOUR MOHAIR FELLOW
Answer: When Mom saw the toddler's art, she was—"OFF THE WALL"

92. **Jumbles:** BOOTH CRESS AROUSE CORNER
Answer: What the teacher took before he entered the demolition race—A "CRASH" COURSE

93. **Jumbles:** WAFER VISOR OPENLY CONVEX
Answer: Important to do for a young cowboy—LEARN THE "ROPES"

94. **Jumbles:** HENCE UNIFY GUIDED RECTOR
Answer: When she married the famous celebrity, she was—"RE-NOUNED"

95. **Jumbles:** OAKEN AGATE VENDOR HINDER
Answer: The couple visited the nature camp because they had—NOTHING "ON"

96. **Jumbles:** WHILE SINGE EXHALE ARTERY
Answer: This can lead to the altar—THE AISLE

97. **Jumbles:** WHINE OLDER PEPTIC UNSEAT
Answer: Why the play didn't have a long run—IT WAS "PEDESTRIAN"

98. **Jumbles:** FOCUS SCARY BUTLER WEDGED
Answer: What you can do at first, if you're the boss' son—SUCCEED

99. **Jumbles:** DALLY PRUNE JITNEY BUSILY
Answer: Most brides look stunning, but some grooms are—STUNNED

100. **Jumbles:** OXIDE MINUS NEPHEW AFLOAT
Answer: The cross-country trucker stayed thin when he watched this—THE "FEED" LIMIT

101. **Jumbles:** TWEAK HIKER MATURE PARDON
Answer: When the wealthy matron was caught shoplifting, she found it—HARD TO "TAKE"

102. **Jumbles:** SKIMP ENVOY UNHOLY BUCKLE
Answer: What the comedian gave the heckler—A "PUNCH" LINE

103. **Jumbles:** FLAME ANNUL MODEST CHEERY
Answer: This helps construction workers bond—CEMENT

104. **Jumbles:** MIRTH PAPER VERSUS ZINNIA
Answer: When he won the distinguished gentleman contest, it was a—SIR PRIZE

105. **Jumbles:** SOOTY KITTY UNFOLD ORCHID
Answer: Both gasoline and electricity can do this—"SHOCK" YOU

106. **Jumbles:** SURLY MESSY NOVICE RATHER
Answer: What the shoppers turned up at the perfume counter—THEIR NOSES

107. **Jumbles:** GUISE SNORT TOWARD SEETHE
Answer: Many authors of Halloween books are—"GHOST" WRITERS

108. **Jumbles:** AXIOM APRON IMPUGN MOSQUE
Answer: What she is in an English class?—A PRONOUN

109. **Jumbles:** FLORA HOARD UNLESS HERMIT
Answer: For a dentist, making a living is—HAND TO MOUTH

110. **Jumbles:** ERASE TITLE POTTER GYPSUM
Answer: Unwrapping their treats during the cowboy movie made them —RUSTLERS

111. **Jumbles:** DRAFT ESSAY FLATLY KISMET
Answer: A good way to make money last—MAKE IT FIRST

112. **Jumbles:** BEGOT FRUIT PONDER INJURE
Answer: What the sales clerk did when he first used a calculator—"FIGURED" IT OUT

113. **Jumbles:** FINAL LIVEN VELLUM INCOME
Answer: When the sweethearts slipped on the ice, they—FELL, IN LOVE

114. **Jumbles:** RODEO QUOTA BLUING GAMBLE
Answer: The piano player quit the pop band because he wanted to—GO FOR BAROQUE

115. **Jumbles:** BASIC ROACH SHREWD SALUTE
Answer: This can keep a skin doctor busy—A RASH OF RASHES

116. **Jumbles:** NAÏVE ELATE CALICO UNRULY
Answer: When the drapery salesman visited the theater, it was a—CURTAIN CALL

117. **Jumbles:** FAINT LAUGH FONDLY EXHORT
Answer: A reputation as two-faced made her—FRIEND OR "FAUX"

118. **Jumbles:** ELUDE IMPEL MEADOW HALVED
Answer: When she bought the expensive party shoes, she was—WELL-HEELED

119. **Jumbles:** BRAWL CRANK CHUBBY BEHAVE
Answer: This can keep astronauts on the ground—A LAUNCH BREAK

120. **Jumbles:** CYNIC ODDLY DAMAGE ACCORD
Answer: How to keep a rhino from charging—CANCEL HIS CARD

121. **Jumbles:** GUIDE CRIME ELICIT BARIUM
Answer: What the bride and groom had at their wedding—A "RICE" TIME

122. **Jumbles:** DUSKY CRAZE UNFAIR OUTING
Answer: What a back seat driver seldom seems to do—RUN OUT OF "GAS"

123. **Jumbles:** DEITY CRESS GLOOMY UNTRUE
Answer: What the comedian's funny routine generated—"SERIOUS" MONEY

124. **Jumbles:** COVEY UNWED ALBINO WISELY
Answer: When higher ups appear in gossip columns, readers often get the—LOWDOWN

125. **Jumbles:** FANCY COCOA DEFAME FRIGID
Answer: It's easier to stick to a diet these days if you eat what you—CAN AFFORD

126. **Jumbles:** VIPER KEYED POWDER SHADOW
Answer: The hosts made the visitors feel at home when they—WISHED THEY WERE

127. **Jumbles:** MERCY VIRUS FLEECE EXTENT
Answer: When the skunk drew the crowd's attention, it became the—"SCENTER" OF IT

128. **Jumbles:** MOSSY TWEET NEEDLE BEWARE
Answer: What the waiters turned into on vacation—WADERS

129. **Jumbles:** MILKY DANDY OBJECT SPEEDY
Answer: When they exchanged words in the sauna, things got—"STEAMY"

130. **Jumbles:** CHASM MAKER CHORUS DEPUTY
Answer: Too many beers on the job left the carpenter—"HAMMERED"

131. **Jumbles:** HUSKY BLOOD PICKET IMBUED
Answer: What the fisherman did when his helper was late—"DOCKED" HIM

132. **Jumbles:** THYME GNOME SMOKER BESTOW
Answer: How he felt when his wife bought a big diamond—"STONE" BROKE

133. **Jumbles:** CRUSH PAUSE TRUDGE BEFOUL
Answer: What the bike racer felt when he fixed the flat tire—"PRESSURE"

134. **Jumbles:** HEDGE SOUSE EMBRYO ALWAYS
Answer: What it takes to unveil plans for a new highway—A "ROAD" SHOW

135. **Jumbles:** BATCH LIBEL HUNTER ENGINE
Answer: Why the heavyset homeowner walked to the paint store—TO GET "THINNER"

136. **Jumbles:** WHOOP LANKY GROUCH BECKON
Answer: When the shepherds went fishing, they worked by—HOOK OR BY CROOK

137. **Jumbles:** PRONE GLAND BEWAIL DIGEST
Answer: What the hockey team's dentist did when the player lost some teeth—"BRIDGED" THE GAP

138. **Jumbles:** EPOCH NIPPY WISDOM SMUDGE
Answer: After the boxer lost the fight, he licked—HIS WOUNDS

139. **Jumbles:** MUSIC ARBOR LOCALE POCKET
Answer: What the shoplifter faced when he took the best-seller—A BOOK "CASE"

140. **Jumbles:** SUAVE ALIAS JIGGLE EXCITE
Answer: When the captain raised the periscope, the submarine was at—"SEE" LEVEL

141. **Jumbles:** FLOOR MOUSE GRASSY SHANTY
Answer: What the overworked songstress suffered—SONG STRESS

142. **Jumbles:** FLOUT OFTEN DEAFEN THRIVE
Answer: Mom didn't answer the phone because she was—ON THE "LINE"

143. **Jumbles:** MADLY FAIRY TRICKY ENGULF
Answer: What the sculptor was known for—HIS FEAT OF CLAY

144. **Jumbles:** MOUNT FRAME DECEIT OBLIGE
Answer: A model with a nice figure can get this—
A NICE FIGURE

145. **Jumbles:** AWOKE LLAMA CAMPER FIRING
Answer: What the hired hand cultivated to get ahead—
THE FARMER

146. **Jumbles:** MAJOR CHANT FOURTH SPRUCE
Answer: When the skin doctor opened his practice, he started—FROM "SCRATCH

147. **Jumbles:** OBESE GULCH JAILED SUBTLY
Answer: What the bride did at the makeup table—
SHE "BLUSHED"

148. **Jumbles:** WIPED TRULY FABLED HANGER
Answer: What happened when both employees wanted the last cup of coffee—A FIGHT "BREWED"

149. **Jumbles:** RANCH GLEAM TACKLE BLUISH
Answer: When the sports fan's big-screen TV was repossessed, he suffered—A "SET BACK"

150. **Jumbles:** EXUDE TWICE TONGUE BRAZEN
Answer: What the diving instructor did to keep his business afloat—WENT "UNDER"

151. **Jumbles:** PIKER CHESS VANDAL HITHER
Answer: Why he insisted that his family wear seat belts—
TO SAVE HIS KIN

152. **Jumbles:** ADULT IDIOM SNITCH GHETTO
Answer: She wasn't a good cook, but she was good at this—
"DISHING" IT OUT

153. **Jumbles:** ADAPT JOLLY BECOME ADVICE
Answer: What the locksmith did when he thought he heard gunfire—HE "BOLTED"

154. **Jumbles:** MIDGE NOTCH NINETY UPTOWN
Answer: In the times of tight budgets, staying within means—DOING WITHOUT

155. **Jumbles:** SILKY PARCH PARLOR FORMAT
Answer: Although skiing is popular in wintertime, it can be—A "FALL" SPORT

156. **Jumbles:** MEALY POUCH TETHER WAITER
Answer: What Junior answered when Mom asked how long he'd be gone—THE WHOLE TIME

157. **Jumbles:** TANGY IVORY FORAGE NIBBLE
Answer: His secretary was good at this—"FILING"

158. **Jumbles:** RUSTY WHEAT STYLUS HARROW
Answer: How the German diner described his meal—
THE WORST WURST

159. **Jumbles:** NOISY VITAL MUFFLE BOTTLE
Answer: A patient foots the bill when a podiatrist does this—
BILLS THE FOOT

160. **Jumbles:** CRAWL CHAFF WALLOP CENSUS
Answer: What the vet made at the racetrack—
"HORSE" CALLS

161. **Jumbles:** QUORUM REDUCE AWEIGH LEGACY VANISH GAMBIT
Answer: Why the street workers put up detour signs—
TO MEND THEIR "WAYS"

162. **Jumbles:** SIPHON LACING ATOMIC PUZZLE PSYCHE OSSIFY
Answer: Why the celebrity bad boy decided to clean the mirror—TO POLISH HIS IMAGE

163. **Jumbles:** RELISH PRYING DABBLE GOVERN SINGLE OUTING
Answer: When the baker's creations were a smash hit, he was—"ROLLING" IN DOUGH

164. **Jumbles:** FIGURE BAUBLE DEBATE ANSWER EMBALM ADVICE
Answer: On a busy night, the versatile chef prepared a—
WIDE "RANGE" OF MEALS

165. **Jumbles:** VENDOR EXTANT KENNEL VESTRY BARREL INFUSE
Answer: What the attorney turned into when he read the will—A "FORTUNE" TELLER

166. **Jumbles:** VERMIN WHENCE ALWAYS OBLIGE SOCIAL GARBLE
Answer: How the mountaineer who took an office job ended up—CLIMBING WALLS

167. **Jumbles:** SHEKEL ENGINE RECTOR FATHOM PIGPEN DUGOUT
Answer: When the passengers took the airport stairs, it was a—NON-STOP "FLIGHT"

168. **Jumbles:** MUSEUM SEAMAN BEDBUG STUDIO CORNEA HEARSE
Answer: What the young cook needed to succeed—
SOME "SEASONING"

169. **Jumbles:** SOCKET FIASCO INLAND LACKEY CRABBY DROWSY
Answer: The baker revealed his top secret recipe on a—"KNEAD" TO KNOW BASIS

170. **Jumbles:** TURTLE SLEEPY BROKER WISELY BUTTER CABANA
Answer: What the museum used to assemble the dinosaur bones—A "SKELETON" CREW

171. **Jumbles:** FELLOW WORTHY MAINLY WISELY ADROIT FRIEZE
Answer: When the desert trekkers saw the oasis, it was—
"WELL" ON THEIR WAY

172. **Jumbles:** MAYHEM BABIED CHERUB BOBBIN DEMISE SMUDGE
Answer: What the obnoxious partygoer left—
MUCH TO BE DESIRED

173. **Jumbles:** STYLUS MASCOT FORMAL BOUNTY RARITY OUTBID
Answer: Stargazing can be good when you do this—
STUDY ASTRONOMY

174. **Jumbles:** BAKING LAUNCH BUZZER NIMBLE GHETTO KISMET
Answer: Wearing a choker can be—"BREATHTAKING"

175. **Jumbles:** BLOODY MUSLIN PALATE ZEALOT RADIAL TERROR
Answer: What it took to buy the yacht—
A BOATLOAD OF MONEY

176. **Jumbles:** PASTRY DARING HUMBLE SNITCH FIXING HUNTER
Answer: They took a mountain vacation because it was—
"HIGH" ON THEIR LIST

177. **Jumbles:** FACTOR GUITAR PURIFY LOCATE COHORT OXYGEN
Answer: The boxer turned census taker was—
OUT FOR THE "COUNT"

178. **Jumbles:** BROGUE MALTED GUZZLE CEMENT GIGOLO URCHIN
Answer: What the lawyer did when he hollered at the judge— "COURTED" TROUBLE

179. **Jumbles:** BIGAMY INFANT VERIFY RENEGE ACCEDÈ SHANTY
Answer: She always wore this outfit for the hunt because it was her—RIDING "HABIT"

180. **Jumbles:** INVERT TOTTER BEAGLE SAFARI FUSION MEMOIR
Answer: Sometimes developed when you borrow money—
FORGETFULNESS

Need More Jumbles®?

Order any of these books through your bookseller or call Triumph Books toll-free at 800-335-5323.